The Stages of Our Spiritual Journey

THE PRACTICE OF *A COURSE IN MIRACLES*

The Stages of Our
Spiritual Journey

KENNETH WAPNICK, Ph.D.

Foundation for A COURSE IN MIRACLES®

Foundation for A COURSE IN MIRACLES®
41397 Buecking Drive
Temecula, CA 92590
www.facim.org

Copyright 2009 by the
Foundation for A COURSE IN MIRACLES®

First printing, 2009
Second printing, 2014

Printed in the United States of America

Library of Congress Cataloging-in-Publication Data

Wapnick, Kenneth, 1942-
    The stages of our spiritual journey / Kenneth Wapnick.
        p. cm.
    Book is based on a 2004 workshop.
    Includes bibliographical references and index.
    ISBN 978-1-59142-441-3
    1. Course in Miracles. 2. Spiritual biography. 3. Nietzsche,
Friedrich Wilhelm, 1844-1900. I. Title.
        BP605.C68W3599 2009
        299'.93--dc22   2009014851

CONTENTS

Preface

The 2004 workshop on which this book is based was entitled, simply, "On the Three Metamorphoses." When we put it out as a CD, the title was expanded to read: "'On the Three Metamorphoses': Nietzsche, *A Course in Miracles*, and the Stages of Spirituality." We reverted to simplicity in title for this book, *The Stages of Our Spiritual Journey*—another in the series "The Practice of *A Course in Miracles*"—as the specific focus is on the stages we go through on our pathway home. Nietzsche's brilliant fable, which can be read straight through in the Appendix, provides the framework for our discussion, on which I elaborate in the introductory chapters.

At the same time that *A Course in Miracles* emphasizes the non-dualistic nature of reality, which is infinite and eternal, beyond our experiential categories of space and time (opposite sides of the ego's illusion of separation—T-26.VIII.1:3-5), we are also told that our journey is a *process* occurring over time. Thus we do not go directly from illusion to truth, but need to take the "little steps" (W-pI.193.13:7) that will lead us to our goal. These steps constitute the stages of our spiritual path, and Nietzsche's "On the Three Metamorphoses" offers a most helpful way of conceptualizing the journey. It is my hope that this book will help students understand the process of forgiveness more fully as it is expressed in their lives, that it be a source of encouragement and hope as they struggle with undoing their identification with the ego thought system of separation and specialness.

As is our usual practice, we have edited the transcript of the original workshop so that it would be more reader friendly. Questions and answers that were irrelevant to the book's theme have been removed, while several others were reframed and inserted into the general flow of the discussion. Throughout, we have striven to preserve the relative informality of the workshop.

Finally, in addition to Nietzsche's fable, the Appendix includes two other pieces to which I refer in my discussion: Helen Schucman's poem "A Jesus Prayer," and the "Development of Trust" section from the manual for teachers, which presents Jesus' description of the six stages of development of the advanced teachers of God.

Acknowledgments

I am deeply grateful to Rosemarie LoSasso, the Foundation's Director of Publications, for her invaluable help in preparing the book from the original workshop, and faithfully shepherding its journey through its various stages. As always, my wife

Gloria's editorial assistance in reading the book was most helpful, a clear reflection of her ongoing inspiration in my life and work. My love and gratitude to her is beyond all stages, and reaches to Heaven.

1. Introduction: Friedrich Nietzsche

The topic of this book, once again, is the stages on our spiritual journey. The framework is the writings of Friedrich Nietzsche, specifically the section "On the Three Metamorphoses" from his masterpiece, *Thus Spoke Zarathustra*. I have two reasons for doing this: The first is personal. I have always appreciated Nietzsche's brilliant insights and literary style, and this is a welcomed opportunity to talk about him and his work. The second reason, and a more important one, is that his wonderful fable provides us with an incisive summary of the spiritual path, parallel to the Course's view, as we shall see presently. Moreover, it is helpful for students of *A Course in Miracles* to have some idea of its intellectual context—psychologically, philosophically, and spiritually. It can be enlightening for those interested in the Course to read about ideas that were written long before its scribing, observing that some of the insights have been around for millennia. *A Course in Miracles*, therefore, did not appear out of nowhere, for intellectually it is a part of a long tradition, with some illustrious people as forebears. And so, once we become familiar with the Course's principles and then read Nietzsche's work, we will be astonished at the pearls of wisdom found in this 19th-century genius.

1. Introduction: Friedrich Nietzsche

Freud said of Nietzsche that he had a more penetrating knowledge of himself than any man who ever lived or who is ever likely to live, an extraordinary statement coming from the father of psychoanalysis. Nietzsche, who lived from 1844 to 1900, actually began his work with his own self-analysis. Freud, who was twelve years his junior, read a lot of Nietzsche when he was a young man and decided he would never read him again. In his words, Nietzsche was "too rich," by which he meant that he was aware that Nietzsche was saying the same kinds of things that he, at that point early in his life, was merely intuiting. Freud also recognized the importance of coming to similar conclusions in his own way, thereby being able to develop his own science of psychoanalysis. He thought that reading too much of Nietzsche would interfere with that process. Thus, while he had tremendous respect for Nietzsche, as is clear from the above statement, he really did not study him. Interestingly, several sessions of a psychoanalytic congress held in 1907 or 1908 were devoted to Nietzsche, and it was during one of those sessions that Freud made the comment about his German ancestor.

One of the key psychoanalytic concepts, the *id*, Freud's term for the unconscious, actually comes from Nietzsche (indirectly through Freud's younger associate, Georg Groddeck). Nietzsche wrote about the unconscious and called it *It*, which in German is *Es*. He described the unconscious the way Freud did—wild, unbridled, and yet a force that had tremendous influence on our lives. Freud's English translators, instead of translating *Es* as *It*, used the Latin *id* to make psychoanalysis appear more scientific.

Nietzsche's influence was extraordinary, not only on Freud but on many, many others. He could even be called the father of existentialism. The famous statement "God is dead," popular in the 1960s and 1970s and, to some extent even today, was Nietzschean.

I conclude this introduction with a brief summary of Nietzsche's life. His father was part of a long line of Lutheran pastors, and died when Friedrich was four or five. However, his father's influence was strong, and in his early years Friedrich was deeply religious and actually studied theology. From all accounts he was a very good little boy, an obedient child who did everything he was told to do. He had gone to a strict private school, and there is a story that reflects this trait of absolute obedience. The pupils were instructed to walk to and from school in a slow, measured pace. One day there was a thunderstorm, and our little friend walked home as he was told to do, not running or seeking shelter. He thus returned home thoroughly drenched. This kind of behavior is in marked contrast to his later, iconoclastic life.

Friedrich was raised by his mother and two aunts, and his brilliance led to his being sent away to a school where he would study theology and philology (the study of the classics). However, he quickly abandoned theology, and for the remainder of his life was a vociferous if not virulent critic of Christianity, indeed of all organized religion. He believed that it corrupted people's morals and kept them in an inferior position. He once spoke of priests as weak men who led even weaker people.

Nietzsche was a master of the German language. Walter Kaufmann, a great Nietzschean scholar and translator, said of him that he was one of the few philosophers since Plato, which means including Plato, whom large numbers of intelligent people read for pleasure, unlike, for example, philosophers like Aristotle, Hegel, or Kant. Nietzsche often wrote in an aphoristic style, meaning that his writings are replete with aphorisms, sayings, fables, parables, and stories. This makes for easy reading, as the reader does not have to wade through a great deal of intellectualism, something Nietzsche abhorred. Incidentally, that is why, in many academic circles, Nietzsche was never regarded as a philosopher in the usual sense.

Majoring in philology, Nietzsche received his doctorate at the early age of twenty-four, unheard of in those years, and was named professor of philology at the University of Basel in Switzerland. Shortly afterward, he came in contact with the great composer, Richard Wagner. Wagner was the same age as Nietzsche's father, and for about ten years the elder man became a parental surrogate to Nietzsche, who also was a great lover of the composer's music dramas. It is of note that in his student days, Nietzsche composed several pieces, none of which I think have survived. He had great respect for Wagner, whom he saw as the hope of German culture, a position he later repudiated.

Nietzsche's first major work was a highly influential book called *The Birth of Tragedy* (1872). He talked about tragedy as an art form, beginning with the ancient Greeks, whom he essentially dismissed on the grounds that they, and he included Socrates and Plato in this category, were too rational and neglected the emotional side of life. This reflected the distinction between Apollo and Dionysus that Friedrich Schiller, a prominent German poet, was the first to describe. The Apollonian represents the intellectual and logical, while Dionysius represents the impulsive and emotional. Nietzsche felt the Greeks came down heavily on the side of the former, and Richard Wagner was an example of the latter, the one who resurrected the tragedy and gave it back its emotion.

Nietzsche began breaking with Wagner when he was around thirty years of age, in part because he felt his former mentor had sold out to Christianity. This was not the case, but nonetheless was how Nietzsche saw it. However, it was really more of a psychological rupture. Wagner was a man who allowed only one genius in his household, and so there was no room for this intellectually precocious young man who was his protege. Wagner could not stand the idea of his brilliant "son" being as brilliant, if not more so, than he, and so Nietzsche had to escape this suffocating environment. However, though he broke with Wagner, Nietzsche never stopped writing about him—positively as well as negatively—up to the end of his life. And he always remained a champion of Wagner's music.

Among Nietzsche's other major books are *Beyond Good and Evil* (1886), *The Genealogy of Morals* (1887), and *The Case of Wagner* (1888). His final book *Ecce Homo*, written in 1888 but not published until well after his death in 1908, reviews and discusses all his writings. The title was taken from the Latin words in John's gospel that Pontius Pilate is said to have uttered when he presented Jesus: "Here is the man"—*Ecce homo*. Because Nietzsche did not think much of Jesus, certainly not the biblical figure, taking that as a title was a statement that Jesus was not the man, *he* was.

Nietzsche was a sickly person, in continual poor health and in tremendous pain. He suffered from severe migraine headaches and his eyesight was impaired. His physicians urged him not to read or write more than one hour a day, if that; however, he generally spent nine to ten hours a day working and was always suffering. Indeed, in *Thus Spoke Zarathustra,* his hero talks about the importance of suffering and not denying it, because it becomes a motivation for moving beyond it. Zarathustra, needless to say, is Nietzsche's alter ego, his spokesman as it were.

In 1889, Nietzsche collapsed on a street in Turin, Italy, and rapidly descended into insanity. The last eleven years of his life he spent doing absolutely nothing. He lived with his mother, and when she died, his sister Elisabeth took care of him until his death in 1900. There are many theories about his insanity, but the cause that scholars consider the most plausible is syphilis, which he probably contracted as a student during a rare (if not only) visit to a bordello. The untreated disease took many years to progress, and finally took its toll in 1889 when the insanity overtook him.

His sister was an important figure in the public life of Nietzsche. She was a proto-Nazi (a Nazi before there was National Socialism), and married a man who later became an active member of the Nazi party when it came to power. She believed in the supremacy of the Aryan people and used her brother's works as support for her beliefs in a master race. Indeed, Elisabeth was responsible for a large number of serious misunderstandings of Nietzsche's work—leading, probably, to the Nazi embrace of Nietzsche, thinking he was really writing for them. In actuality, they totally misunderstood everything he wrote, which again was largely because of Elisabeth, who edited his works after he became insane and corrupted a number of his significant concepts. Being the owner of his *oeuvre*, she decided what was to be published after editing out what she did not like and keeping what she did.

It was not until many years later that people were able to go back to the original writings and discover that Nietzsche did not write what Elisabeth claimed he did. For example, he spoke of the *overman,* which in German is *Übermensch* (*über* meaning "over" and *mensch* meaning "man")—a key concept in *Thus Spoke Zarathustra.* It is similar to what *A Course in Miracles* calls an "advanced teacher of God"*— someone who is able to transcend or move beyond both the animal and human kingdoms and transcend

---

* See for example, M-4.1:6; 2:2; M-4.VI.1:6; M-16.1:1; 9:5.

the body. Nietzsche did not mean this in the Course sense of recognizing the illusory nature of the corporeal, but more that the *Übermensch* would no longer be bound by the world's customs and values. Elisabeth interpreted this highly important concept to mean *superman*, which well served the Nazi doctrine of the master (or super) race. Indeed, many of the early English versions of Nietzsche translated the German as *superman*. However, it is quite obvious what Nietzsche meant, because he contrasted the *Übermensch* with the word *unter*, meaning "under." Thus he would say, for example, that when you "go under," you go into the world, and he obviously enjoyed the word play of *unter* and *über*. It is patently clear that he did not mean *super* at all.

Another important concept in Nietzsche's thinking was the *will to power,* by which he meant spiritual power: we become what we really can be—the *Übermensch*. Once again, however, a significant Nietzschean concept was taken by Elisabeth as something material and militaristic, embracing great physical strength, then used by the Nazis almost as a slogan. The negative assessments of Nietzsche often have their roots in these misconceptions. Everything this profound thinker wrote needs to be understood within a spiritual context. This will become even clearer as we go through "On the Three Metamorphoses."

Nietzsche's work was not discovered and appreciated until after he died, and not many copies were made of his writings. Hardly known at the time, these writings needed the influential literary figure Stephen Zweig, contemporary of Thomas Mann and also a "Nietzschean," to discover them and to champion Nietzsche and his work.

2. The Stages of Spirituality: Introduction

We turn now to *Thus Spoke Zarathustra*, perhaps Nietzsche's most popular work, and "On the Three Metamorphoses."* Zarathustra was the great Persian visionary and prophet (c.628–c.551 B.C.) whose ideas were dominant in Western Asia until about A.D. 650, and are still held by thousands in India and the rest of Asia. Not much is known about him, other than that he was the founder of Zoroastrianism (the Greek for *Zarathrustra*), one of the world's clearest expressions of dualism—good and evil are both real in the world and, according to Zarathustra, good will ultimately triumph. This was not really Nietzsche's philosophy, but he wanted an ancient spiritual figure as the protagonist of his book. Again, Nietzsche did not think highly of Jesus, whom he saw as a failure, dying much too early to have accomplished anything. Moreover, he did not like what Christianity did with him. Zarathustra was therefore a more familiar and comfortable figure. The book is in four parts. The first three were essentially written within a year or so of each other, and each part was written in about ten days, in a virtual white heat of creativity. These first

---

* All quotations are from the translation by Walter Kaufmann (Viking Penguin, 1954).

three sections were published in 1883 and 1884, and the fourth part was completed in 1885 but did not appear until 1892.

As a prelude to our discussion of "On the Three Metamorphoses," I want to comment briefly on a few passages from *Thus Spoke Zarathustra* that give us a flavor of the insights shared by both Nietzsche and *A Course in Miracles*, and that can thus serve as a backdrop for our discussion:

But if you have an enemy, do not requite him evil with good, for that would put him to shame. Rather prove that he did you some good (p. 68).

This can be understood in the context of the section "The Correction of Error" from the text (T-9.III). Nietzsche is telling us not to prove our brother wrong, even though he may be wrong from the world's point of view. Instead, we need to show him that he did us some good. Of course the good, which we understand from our study of *A Course in Miracles*, is that whatever someone has done or has not done to us becomes an opportunity for us to forgive ourselves, and *that* is the good. Therefore, if someone is attacking or insulting us, we would not requite him with evil, or his perceived evil with good. Rather, we would choose to show him he is right because he is a Son of God, as are we. In this way, his perceived attack on us becomes the vehicle for our realizing that happy fact.

Shortly after this, Zarathustra states:

It is nobler to declare oneself wrong than to insist on being right—especially when one is right. Only one must be rich enough for that (p. 68).

In other words, we have to be rich within ourselves (i.e., know our wholeness) to be able to say that we were wrong, even though we may have been right about a specific issue. This is reminiscent of the well-known line from the Course:

> Do you prefer that you be right or happy? (T-29.VII.1:9)

And then there is the following perfectly astonishing statement from earlier in the book that is directly relevant to the Course's teaching of rising "above the battleground" (see T-23.IV). This means that we return to our mind and look back on the world, with Jesus or the Holy Spirit, at which point we see everything differently. Here is what Zarathustra—Nietzsche's mouthpiece—taught:

I no longer feel as you do: this cloud which I see beneath me, this blackness and gravity at which I laugh—this is your thundercloud.

You look up when you feel the need for elevation. And I look down because I am elevated. Who among you can laugh and be elevated at the same time? Whoever climbs the highest mountains laughs at all tragic plays and tragic seriousness (pp. 40-41).

In other words, Zarathustra is saying to his listeners that although they may perceive the world as an ominous thundercloud, from where he is—above the cloud—it deserves only laughter. Although the words here are different, one can see the similarity in content to the Course's "above the battleground." This means that when we have not risen to the level of the mind, where Jesus is, and are thus in the world and identified with the ego thought system of separation and bodies, we will take matters here very seriously. It is only when we are above the clouds and look down that we realize that nothing here is what it seems. Then we can laugh at the "tragic plays and tragic seriousness." Nietzsche's work is replete with these kinds of insights, which again is why Freud made the comments he did, not to mention why he is the favorite philosopher of so many, professional and non-professional alike.

As with Nietzsche's other works, *Thus Spoke Zarathustra* is not a philosophical treatise. It begins with a prologue that sets the stage. Zarathustra, at the age of 30, goes into the mountains and lives there for 10 years by himself, where he reaches many of his insights. By the way, Zarathustra, while obviously an advanced spiritual soul, is not enlightened. He clearly knows a great deal more than most, but he has not reached the highest level of spiritual attainment. He could thus be likened to an advanced teacher of God (see p. 8 above). This also is reflective of Nietzsche's state.

Returning to the world, Zarathustra begins to teach about the *overman*, Nietzsche's name for one who is spiritually enlightened (the advanced teacher of God), as we have just seen. Further along in the course of his travels, Zarathustra comes across a tightrope walker who falls off the tightrope, dies, and is left there on the ground. Zarathustra feels it is his duty to carry him, which he does for many miles in order to give him a proper burial. He finally buries him in the hollow of a tree, and then says: "An insight has come to me: companions I need, living ones—not dead companions and corpses whom I carry with myself wherever I want to" (p. 23). Zarathustra's statement is a symbol for living in the present and not carrying around the past, represented by the dead, paralleling these lines from the workbook:

> Be still today and listen to the truth. Be not deceived by voices of the dead, which tell you they

> have found the source of life and offer it to you
> for your belief. Attend them not, but listen to the
> truth (W-pI.106.2:2-4).

The teacher then goes to another village, which ends the prologue, and there he begins his teaching on the three metamorphoses. This sets the stage for the rest of the book's four parts. Nietzsche continually refers back to these three parts of the spiritual life.

Let me briefly describe the three stages, and then we will begin a line-by-line commentary, showing the similarities of each stage with the teaching in *A Course in Miracles*. The three stages are the *camel,* the *lion,* and the *child.*

The *camel,* the beginning stage of one's journey, depicts what it means to grow up in the world. Nietzsche is quite clear that one does not become a lion, let alone a child, without first being a camel, which means learning how to be in the world.

The next stage is the *lion,* who then realizes that everything the world has taught is false. The stage of the lion, which basically reflects where Nietzsche was, is to see the falsity of the world and to let it know that—in other words, to say no to the world. Then Zarathustra makes it clear that that is not the end of the journey, because there still has to be the final creative yes.

For that, the *child* is needed. For Nietzsche, the child is the symbol of innocence, and the counterpart to what we find in Lesson 182 in the workbook—the Child in us who wants to go home. It is not the image of a child that Jesus usually refers to throughout the Course, where he calls us little children who do not know anything. For Nietzsche, the child is the symbol of innocence and a new beginning. It is the vision that Jesus holds out to us as the happy effect of having moved beyond the darkness of our egos into the light of forgiveness.

3. Stage One: The Camel

As a point of clarification, the word *spirit* in this piece could be translated as *mind,* although in German there is no word for *mind*; the word *geist* (which means *spirit*) is typically used instead. It is obvious, as we shall see, that since Nietzsche is talking about the evolution of spirit, he is not talking about our spiritual self, which is changeless and eternal, but about the split (or decision-making) mind on its journey.

Of the three metamorphoses of the spirit I tell you: how the spirit becomes a camel; and the camel, a lion; and the lion, finally, a child.[*]

These are the three stages. We can make a rough comparison between these stages and the six stages described in "Development of Trust"[†] in the manual for teachers (M-4.I), except that in *A Course in Miracles* the first four stages have to do with the lion, not the camel. There is really nothing in the Course that deals with the camel, for reasons that I will explain shortly. Helen's poem "A Jesus Prayer,"[**] which begins with the lines "A Child, a Man and then a Spirit," could be

---

[*] All quotations are from the translation by Walter Kaufmann (Viking Penguin, 1954), pp. 25-27.
[†] Reprinted in the Appendix.
[**] *The Gifts of God*, pp. 82-83; reprinted in the Appendix.

seen as roughly comparable to what Nietzsche is talking about. The child is the camel, the man is the lion, and the spirit would be Nietzsche's child.

There is much that is difficult for the spirit, the strong reverent spirit that would bear much: but the difficult and the most difficult are what its strength demands.

Nietzsche is saying that there is much that is difficult for us on our journey. What we are asked to do, as we know from our study of the Course, is to let go of the ego. This is what is "difficult and the most difficult" because the resistance to being without our specialness is so strong.

Here, now, is the first stage. I will present it in Nietzsche's terms, and then discuss its meaning and implications for our work with *A Course in Miracles*.

What is difficult? asks the spirit that could bear much, and kneels down like a camel wanting to be well loaded. What is most difficult, O heroes, asks the spirit that would bear much, that I may take it upon myself and exult in my strength? Is it not humbling oneself to wound one's haughtiness? Letting one's folly shine to mock one's wisdom?

Nietzsche is talking about the highly important concept of humility: "humbling oneself to wound one's haughtiness." Haughtiness, of course, is a phenomenon almost universally found in adolescents and young adults who think they know everything and that the world has nothing to teach them. Recall the famous exclamation from an earlier generation that no one over thirty should be trusted because what they know is already irrelevant. Zarathustra is saying that you humble yourself so that you can learn. "Letting one's folly shine to mock one's wisdom" is to realize how much we do not know—the folly of our thinking and of our living—which then ends up mocking what we think to be our wisdom. Since no one over thirty knows anything that is still relevant, why read anything of theirs? Philosophers, psychologists, theologians, and the like are but stuffy old-fashioned people who do not understand what the world is really like. The clear implication of Zarathustra's words is that if we do not learn how to live within the ego thought system, if we do not feel comfortable with our ego, body, or world, we can never move beyond them.

It is interesting that Nietzsche himself reached that point. He went through the stage of the camel; being an obedient student, he learned and studied. Only then was he able to say that it all made no sense. His own life became a wonderful example of how one begins as a camel and ends as a lion, rejecting the world's values. He does not really become a child, however. Although he has intimations of what that stage means, it is obvious that he himself never got there. He is a man on the journey, well along the path, and wiser than the people he is speaking to, but he is not there yet and does not claim to be. One could liken Nietzsche to Moses, standing on the mountain and seeing the promised land beyond the river, but not able to cross over. Nietzsche described this land, knew it was there, but remained outside it. He was clear, however, about what it meant to be a lion, and that one could not be one without first becoming a camel. Later we will discuss the implications of this for our study of *A Course in Miracles*.

Nietzsche now lists characteristics—"Or is it this...?"—that he says are part of the humbling process. We can see these through the lens of the Course, learning how to be an ego and how to live in the world. We do not deny the ego until we first know we have one. We do not say we are not a body until we first know we have one and are comfortable with it. If we flee from the body, being unable to deal with our physical and psychological needs, how could we ever satisfactorily and truly get beyond it? We would always be operating out of fear and guilt, which only serve to make the body real in our experience. What we despise is every bit as real as what we love: aversion and attraction are but two sides of the same coin of the body's seeming reality.

Or is it this: parting from our cause when it triumphs? Climbing high mountains to tempt the tempter?

Humility means, in part, that we would not build monuments to our successes. Nietzsche is talking about not resting on one's laurels. For example, if you are a student and pass a course, get an A, or attain a degree, you leave your accomplishment behind and move on. We should not have the illusion of "being there" when we are not. This does not preclude climbing high mountains: striving for success, having goals and achieving them. Rather, this is about the formative years we all go through, when we learn how to live in the world and have aspirations—educational, vocational, and personal. The problem is never the goals or what we have attained, but our investment in them, using worldly accomplishments as a form of specialness, their purpose being to substitute idols of love and self-worth for the genuine feeling of dignity and peace that only comes from the acceptance of our right minds.

This is why *A Course in Miracles* is not for children, or for grown children either. It is for those who have attained a certain level of maturity—social, physical, and psychological—and have more or less made it in the world. They have climbed the high mountains and developed their egos in the world's sense, which is what it means to "tempt the tempter." They do not stay there, though, because they realize that the mountain they have just scaled is simply part of a larger and more glorious mountain range—so they do not stop. That is humility. They achieve their worldly and personal goals, but do not stop with them because if they do, they will end up with nothing: life in the ego's desert of guilt, fear, and specialness.

Or is it this: feeding on the acorns and grass of knowledge and, for the sake of the truth, suffering hunger in one's soul?

In other words, we are always wanting more, not being satisfied with what we have. We seek knowledge, but realize there is always something additional to learn. The wisdom of the young is knowing there is much more to learn—that the present is just a stage leading toward something else. *Young* thus refers to those who have not attained the level of maturity that would allow them to take the next step of renouncing everything they had heretofore learned. We cannot move to the next stage if we are not faithful to the requirements of the camel—of bearing the burdens of the world. Recall the popular expression, "paying your dues," which means we do not presume to be wiser or more spiritually advanced than we are. We cannot say no to the ego, and we cannot say, as the workbook states over and over again, "I am not a body," unless we first go through the stages of believing we *are* a body and *have* an ego. Otherwise we would be heavily into denial, hardly a spiritual state. This is one reason Nietzsche's thought is profoundly important and his work so insightful: he recognized the need for growth.

Or is it this: being sick and sending home the comforters and making friends with the deaf, who never hear what you want?

We come to realize that we do not want to be focusing always on self-indulgence, having our needs met, or having people feel sorry for us. We send home the people who would comfort and feel sorry for us, or stroke us and thereby keep us down by reinforcing our self-image of inadequacy. What we truly want are people who meet us where we are, and then help us to grow. We want people who would be deaf to our self-indulgences, specialness demands, and temper tantrums. This is how we begin to reflect the wisdom that only comes much later, when we, in Nietzsche's fable, become a child.

Or is it this: stepping into filthy waters when they are the waters of truth, and not repulsing cold frogs and hot toads?

The spiritual life is hard work. We have to delve into the murky depths of our psyche, the pits of the ego: "stepping into filthy waters when they are the waters of truth, and not repulsing cold frogs and hot toads." Typically, so many people on a spiritual path, including students of *A Course in Miracles*, do not want to get their hands dirty at all with the ego. These are what we commonly refer to as "blissninnies," people who cover over everything negative. That is what Jesus means when he says that the Holy Spirit will walk with us through "seeming terror" to our God Who is beyond it (T-18.IX.3:7-9). The "seeming terror" is the ego's thought system of guilt and judgment, the "filthy waters... [of] cold frogs and hot toads."

This, then, is why we are here and why we made up a world and body: to keep God out (W-pII.3.2:4). And so before we can forgive the ego and what it has done with our body and the bodies of others, we first have to know what our minds have done, or believe they have done. We have to learn that our self is not a pristine, beautiful, and innocent child—it is a "hot toad" and "cold frog." The waters of the wrong mind are murky and filthy. Thus we need these formative years of our life, when we study and become something, or at least become somewhat experienced in such areas as interpersonal relations, education, vocation, earning money, and perhaps having a partner and raising a family. This means getting our hands dirty by dealing with the nitty gritty of being in the body, living in

> a dry and dusty world, where starved and thirsty creatures come to die (W-pII.13.5:1).

To avoid this is to avoid what in the end would strengthen us. We therefore cannot become lions until we first become camels and bear the burden of what it means to be living here.

Or is it this: loving those who despise us and offering a hand to the ghost that would frighten us?

Thus Spoke Zarathustra is replete with biblical allusions, as is true of many other Nietzsche works. As we saw above, Nietzsche studied the Bible in his early years, and although he rejected its teaching, he certainly knew what it said. In the Sermon on the Mount, Jesus said that we should love those who despise or hate us (Matthew 5:44), and Nietzsche is saying we should not only love those who despise us, but also offer a hand to the ghost that would frighten us. In other words, embrace *everything* that happens here. This is an essential part of his philosophy.

The concept of *eternal recurrence* is probably the most important concept in all of Nietzsche's work;

yet, paradoxically, it is rarely referred to. It is mentioned in *The Gay Science* (1882), a book he wrote just before *Zarathustra*. When Zarathustra talks about it in Part Three, it is with great trepidation, almost as if he is afraid to even say the words. In fact, in one place he does not say them; the animals he always travels with do. His two most important companions are the eagle and snake; the eagle because it sees everything and is proud, and the snake because it is wise. It is therefore his animals who preach to him about *eternal recurrence*, the idea that every single thing that has happened and is happening to us now will happen again and again and again. Even the smallest detail will continually recur. In one passage, for example, Nietzsche even says that the spider crawling in the moonlight will keep crawling and crawling. This idea, obviously quite frightening to Nietzsche, was used by him as a litmus test to see how spiritually advanced people were; how comfortable or uncomfortable they were with this concept. He did not really develop it in his thinking, which goes to the heart of the problem—Nietzsche's inability to integrate it within his philosophy or personal life.

We can apply the Course's view of time to Nietzsche's view of *eternal recurrence*. In *A Course in Miracles*, Jesus teaches us that since everything has already happened, we are merely "reviewing mentally what has gone by" (W-pI.158.3,4; T-28.I.1:6), watching, as it were, old videos. This idea, and we can assume that this is what frightened Nietzsche, is really saying that nothing here is meaningful (cf. the early workbook lessons).

The *overman*, once again, is Nietzsche's spiritual ideal: we do not avoid what happens, but embrace it; we embrace as well the people who despise us and the events that frighten us. We do not try to avoid what is on our plate because, as the Course would teach, that would ensure its happening over and over unceasingly. Nietzsche is saying that we need to raise ourselves above the cloud (the Course's "battleground"), thereby freeing ourselves to no longer see the world as tragic and serious. Thus we would eventually learn how to laugh at what goes on. Recall Jesus' words from the text:

> It is not easy to perceive the jest when all around you do your eyes behold its heavy consequences, but without their trifling cause. Without the cause do its effects seem serious and sad indeed. Yet they but follow. And it is their cause that follows nothing and is but a jest (T-27.VIII.8:4-7).

The *cause* is our mind's belief in the sin of separation, which in reality never happened. In other words, we become aware of the "eternal" recurrence of everything, which the Course helps us to understand as the "eternal" recurrence of the ego thought system that transcends time and space. It is not linear, so of course the same thing happens over and over again as long as we remain asleep. We therefore are always watching very old reruns. The challenge, though, is to move beyond the ego's thought system without denying it.

This, in a sense, is how Nietzsche dealt with his own suffering. He was in pain constantly, but rather than avoid it—he did take medication for it—he felt he should embrace his lot in life and not flee from it. He is not talking about deliberately bringing suffering onto oneself or being a masochist, but rather about accepting whatever the script is, and then learning to look at it differently. This is the task of the camel. It acquires the tools for survival in the material world of physical and psychological bodies: learning to get along with others and to deal with life's basics—food, shelter, sexuality, emotions, education, and gaining the various skills and abilities necessary for the process of earning a living and surviving here.

Jung also was a great admirer of Nietzsche. He spoke of two main stages in life: the first half essentially belongs to the camel, although Jung of course did not use that image; the second commences when one begins to look at everything from a spiritual point of view. Jung did not give a precise cutoff point, but he held that during our first thirty or thirty-five years we master living in the world, and only after that can we satisfactorily move beyond it. We cannot run until we can walk, and we cannot walk until we can crawl. It takes tremendous humility to be able to say to oneself: "I am not there yet, but this is the period in my life when I will learn how to deal with my body and its relationship to other bodies and to the world. I will be a camel. I will have achievements and goals, but will not remain with them because I know that I am on a journey, and this is only part of it." This, then would be the reflection of wisdom found in a younger person; intuitively knowing that what one is doing is part of something larger. Yet, to make this important point again, we cannot truly understand this larger perspective until we first pay our dues. This sense of humility is what best characterizes Nietzsche's meaning of being a camel—the humility of living in the world, learning from it, and growing within it, without prematurely trying to spiritualize things.

This is why *A Course in Miracles* is not for people who are still struggling with their physical and psychological identities. The danger lies in there being a strong tendency to use the Course as a means of *denying* one's ego rather than *looking* at it. We cannot let go of our ego until we first know that we have one. And so, again, we spend the first part of our life developing and dealing with the ego and our bodily needs; it would make no sense, in the face of the natural developmental issues we all confront, to somehow say that this is an illusion, that we are minds, not bodies, and besides, we are not even here. These metaphysical teachings from the Course mean nothing to us at this early stage. On the other hand, they would mean everything when we reach the stage of Nietzsche's child, which is the end of the process. Once again, this phase of the journey requires great humility.

One of my favorite stories about humility relates to Bruno Walter, a titan among 20th-century conductors. His Beethoven, Schubert, and Brahms were wonderful, his Mahler out of this world, and his Wagner exceptional. But Mozart was the composer closest to his heart. When you listen to a Walter performance of Mozart, you can hear the love like in no other. During an interview he gave near the end of his life, this great conductor said that he could not fathom the young conductors who conducted music they did not understand. Of himself he said that he waited until he was fifty years old—a long time for a musician—before he dared to conduct Mozart's Symphony No. 40 in G Minor. There is a profound sadness in this music, and one great music critic in fact spoke of the symphony as Mozart's Gethsemane, depicting a desolate experience usually absent in Mozart's work. Walter said he would not have thought of conducting this music publicly until he was mature enough to understand it. He was comparing himself to conductors who conduct anything and everything, with no real understanding of the music's depth, a lack that unfortunately is heard in their performances. This, then, is the humility of which Zarathustra speaks.

It is the same with people who have read the Course once or twice and immediately start teaching or writing about it. I am not saying that people should wait until they are fifty to teach *A Course in Miracles*, but the arrogance of presenting something that is not understood should always be looked at. For example, there have been people who have sought to teach the Course without reading it at all, thinking it was just like another spiritual thought system with which they were familiar. There is an arrogance there that is not part of the camel's life. Remember, it is the camel that bears the burdens of the world that *it* made. It is the world that we chose to come into. From a right-minded point of view, we come here to learn our lessons of forgiveness. Yet we cannot learn lessons unless we have a classroom and a curriculum, let alone a teacher. The classroom and curriculum are our lives and relationships, and that means struggling like everyone else with the body's physical and emotional survival in the world.

At some point, when the world becomes "too much with us," to cite Wordsworth, we say: "There must be another way; there has to be more to life than what I am doing." This is when we fire our teacher and bring in Jesus, reflecting this sentence compounded from *A Course in Miracles*:

> Resign now as your own teacher, for you were badly taught (T-12.V.8:3; T-28.I.7:1).

Then all our skills and aptitudes, as well as our experiences, serve a different purpose and become the classroom in which our new teacher—Jesus—instructs us with the goal of leading us home. If Jesus is going to be our teacher, he needs a textbook to teach from, and this, again, is our life. All our experiences—positive and negative, triumphs and failures—are the tools he needs. In other words, he needs our lives as camels. People who pretend to be innocent, holy, and spiritually advanced are not really desirous of being his pupil, for they feel they have already learned all that there is to know. Jesus does not need pseudo-lions who complain about the apocalypses of the world when they are really terrified of it, all the while making it appear they are not. He cannot help those who portray themselves as spiritual nihilists, stating that nothing here means anything, when they are really guilt-ridden and anxious about a world from which they attempt to flee.

Jesus, therefore, needs people who are true camels. That is why there is absolutely nothing in *A Course in Miracles* about this first stage. His underlying premise is that people who come to his course have already achieved a certain level of psychological, physical, and social maturity. They need not be perfectly mature, but they do have to be at a level of maturity that allows them to read that they are not a body, "the world was made as an attack on God" (W-pII.3.2:1), and, moreover, all this is an illusion—and not resonate to these metaphysical statements for the wrong reason. There is an unspoken assumption in *A Course in Miracles* that people who approach it and seek to make it their spiritual path are already camels. They now realize that they are in the desert—the world *is* the desert—and are ready to look at the world differently, which is the lion's role.

Before we move to the stage of the lion, I want to elaborate a little further on what it means to be comfortable with the ego. This would never be the ego's idea, since it never lets us feel comfortable with itself. Our typical reaction to the ego—whether it is ours or others'—is to *do* something: attack or judge it, feel guilty about it, try to fix, change, heal, embrace, or dismiss it, or even deny it is there. To be comfortable with it, in the framework of Nietzsche's ideas, is to embrace it as part of our experience, which means embrace it as something we have chosen. The key theme in *A Course in Miracles*, the heart of forgiveness, is *looking at the ego*. This means looking at the ego with the Holy Spirit or Jesus, which means *looking at the ego without judgment*. Thus we read:

> Forgiveness... is still, and quietly does nothing. ... It merely looks, and waits, and judges not (W-pII.1.4:1,3).

When confronted with some form of the original error of separation, Jesus urges us in words that quite specifically tell us how to deal with the ego:

> Call it not sin.... Invest it not with guilt.... And above all, *be not afraid of it* (T-18.I.6:7-9).

And so we do not call the ego sinful; we do not feel guilty about it; and we are not afraid of it. This means, again, that we do not attack or change it; and certainly we do not pretend it is not there. We simply accept the ego because we have already chosen it, which then allows us the opportunity to change our minds about our mistaken decision.

A Course in Miracles helps us understand that we have chosen the ego to keep the Love of God away. We thus learn to look at our ego and not take it seriously because in truth we cannot separate from God, though in our delusional state we can believe we have. In other words, we do not give the ego—in us or another—power over that experience of love and peace within us. This idea is a commentary on the very important line in the text:

> Into eternity, where all is one, there crept a tiny, mad idea, at which the Son of God remembered not to laugh (T-27.VIII.6:2).

The problem is that we did take the thought of separation seriously, and forgot to laugh at the insignificance and inherent insanity of this fundamental ego belief. The Holy Spirit's response to the *tiny, mad idea* is the loving and gentle smile that does absolutely nothing, which is why everyone has hated Him and anyone who represents Him. When we do something about the ego or any of its manifestations, we have made it real. By struggling against it and trying to change it, all we do is strengthen its reality for us, which means we will never be free of it. This is why the last stage is not the strong lion, who defiantly opposes the world, but the innocent child.

The laughter Jesus speaks about, it should be noted, is not derisive or dismissive; nor is it the physical experience of laughter. Neither Nietzsche nor Jesus means laughing in the literal sense. Physical laughter might be an expression of the inner laughing, but they are referring to not seeing what goes on around or within us as having power to take away the love and peace in our minds. This means that nothing that goes on can be all that serious, our experience often to the contrary, because it cannot change or remove what is most important to us. The laughter is really the Holy Spirit's correction for the ego's taking everything seriously. To stress this important point, we are not talking about physically laughing at someone or at problems. *Laughter* is the word that symbolizes the content of not giving something external power over our minds, thereby undoing the ego's seriousness about a world it has us perceive as real and threatening. Before we can reach that stage, however, we first have to feel comfortable with the ego's world. This is mandatory if we are to make progress.

Thinking of this idea of leaving the ego's world after first becoming comfortable in it, one senses a hint of a major principle of the Buddha: compassion for all sentient beings. This is reflected in *A Course in Miracles'* concept of *true empathy* (T-16.I); you cannot have compassion for anyone unless you have it for *all* beings. It is all or nothing. We have compassion for *all* people or for none of them. Buddha would certainly have agreed, given his belief that this is a world of suffering. If we could do what Zarathustra was saying and elevate above the cloud, we would look at tragedy and laugh—not derisively, but with the attitude of compassion for all who think that they are here, the source of all suffering. Being above the battleground, we recognize that the Sonship is one and that no one is truly separate from us.

The Sonship is one in that we all share the same split mind as well as the same Mind that lies just beyond the separation. Looking down on the world, we recognize that everyone is suffering from the common pain of believing he or she is separate from God and will never be able to return, so beautifully stated at the beginning of Lesson 182 "I will be still an instant and go home." There Jesus talks about the pain of being stuck here as an alien, not knowing how to get home, or even believing there is a home to which we can come back, even if we knew the way. The first part of that lesson expresses the idea that everyone knows what Jesus is speaking about:

> This world you seem to live in is not home to you. And somewhere in your mind you know that this is true. A memory of home keeps haunting you, as if there were a place that called you to return, although you do not recognize the voice, nor what it is the voice reminds you of. Yet still you feel an alien here, from somewhere all unknown. Nothing so definite that you could say with certainty you are an exile here. Just a persistent feeling, sometimes not more than a tiny throb, at other times hardly remembered,

> actively dismissed, but surely to return to mind
> again.
>   No one but knows whereof we speak
> (W-pI.182.1:1–2:1).

Consequently, *everyone* here deserves compassion, because everyone suffers from the same loneliness and alienation. Indeed, the heart of all special relationships, which drives us to seek them one after another, after another, after another, is this deep-seated sense of aloneness. We desperately want the companionship and comfort of another body, magically hoping to dull the mind's pain of being separate from our Source. It was this thought that motivated us at the beginning to make a world, and then to hide as fragments within separate bodies. We all feel the pain, but each of us experiences it differently. Some people camouflage it very well; others do not. However, as long as we identify with being in a body living in this world, we must experience pain. By virtue of having that pain, therefore, everyone deserves compassion. Someone without an ego, even for an instant, let alone someone who has become an advanced teacher or *overman*, would know that pain in all people. How, then, could that person's heart not go out to everyone, not just the good or the bad, but to all people without exception? By the way, the word *man* in German, *mensch*, refers to homo sapiens as a species; it does not denote gender. Thus to be an *overman* means to recognize the essential oneness of all living things (all sentient beings): the Oneness of Christ, and the oneness of believing we are separate from Christ.

To conclude this part of our discussion, let me offer two other models that parallel Nietzsche's teachings and what we learn in *A Course in Miracles*. The first is *Beethoven*, whose life wonderfully represents what Nietzsche is talking about. I mentioned earlier that Nietzsche was a music lover and a musician himself. He cites Beethoven quite a few times in his writing, but does not really discuss him or his music. In fact, Wagner is the only composer he does speak of. On some level, though, he must have known Beethoven's music, and may even have intuitively known that the three periods that characterize his work are a perfect example of the camel, lion, and child.

The first period of Beethoven's music, which essentially constitutes the first thirty-two years of his life, up to 1803, the year of the Third Symphony (the *Eroica*), is an example of a camel. Beethoven paid his dues. To be sure, this is not the period of his greatest music. It consists of the first two piano concertos and symphonies, the first twenty piano sonatas, and the first six string quartets. These are wonderful compositions, but none that would have secured his reputation as one of the world's greatest composers. In this early period, Beethoven's music obeyed the laws and followed the rules of the classical school of Mozart and Haydn. Every once in a while one hears a glimpse of what would come later, but it is fleeting.

Another wonderful example is *Aristotle,* Plato's pupil. These two philosophical giants were at opposite ends of the intellectual spectrum, and in effect form the pillars of Western philosophy. As depicted in Raphael's famous painting "The School of Athens," Plato's philosophy takes us inward, while Aristotle's leads us outward. As majestically brilliant as Aristotle's system is, it remains a system of the world. To his credit, and this is my point here, he remained with Plato until the master's death, and only then did he leave and form his own school and produce his impressive work. In other words, he paid his dues, too. While Plato's influence on his thought is apparent, he went his own way. Yet as far as we know, Aristotle respected his teacher and did not attack the Academy, Plato's school. He learned all he could, and then took his own path, as did Beethoven over two millennia later.

In summary, the stage of the camel is where we learn our craft. We learn about the body and the world, learning whatever is part of our classroom to learn—our script. We do not attempt to jump ahead or dictate spirituality to ourselves, but let it slowly evolve, as it inevitably will. In the same way that one allows a plant to grow at its own pace and all of a sudden it begins to bud, blossoming into a beautiful flower, we do not *make* ourselves spiritual, but rather let the spiritual come to us in its own time, when we are ready.

4. Stage Two: The Lion

At the end of Nietzsche's discussion of humility, he characterized the first stage—learning how to be in the world—as a burden:

All these most difficult things the spirit that would bear much takes upon itself: like the camel that, burdened, speeds into the desert, thus the spirit speeds into its desert.

This takes us to the second stage, wherein the camel, now burdened, goes into the desert, the symbol of the world's aridity, and becomes transformed into the lion. As we have seen, we spend the first part of our life learning how to master the world and our body, learning how to deal with our impulses and needs, and everything physical and psychological that we believe determines who we are. We also learn how to get along with other bodies. All this is part of learning how to be in the world, including earning enough money so we can survive in it. Having completed this stage of our learning, Jung's first half of life, we begin to realize that the world itself is a desert, devoid of true life:

There is no life outside of Heaven (T-23.II.19:1).

In the loneliest desert, however, the second meta-morphosis occurs: here the spirit becomes a lion who would conquer his freedom and be master in his own desert. Here he seeks out his last master: he wants to fight him and his last god; for ultimate victory he wants to fight with the great dragon.

The dragon is the symbol of society and the world, and as Nietzsche will explain, the dragon's body is filled with scales, each of which has on it the words "Thou shalt." Actually, some of the scales could just as easily have said "Thou shalt not." Thus the scales of the great dragon represent everything society and religions say we must do, as well as what we must not do.

Again, the first part of our life is spent learning how to live with the dragon, how to live with the "Thou shalts" of the body: Thou shalt breathe, eat, drink, and learn how to get thy needs met, otherwise thou shalt die. We therefore learn at an early age how to manipulate the adults in our lives so that our needs will be satisfied. Then we grow up and the "Thou shalts" become: Thou shalt go to school, pass courses, learn a trade, develop an ability or skill, and earn money. We then have to decide upon a means of earning money; otherwise we will not be able to purchase food, have a place to live, or obtain clothing.

In the first stage, to paraphrase words from the Course, the world we see offers *something* that we want (W-pI.128)—it offers us survival and the satisfaction of our physical and psychological needs. We are not yet at the point in our development when we have spiritual needs. Just as there are developmental stages in acquiring skills—walking, speaking, using the toilet, and reasoning—there are also developmental stages in spirituality. However, we do not get to those until we first have successfully traversed the earlier ones, which means learning how to live in the world of the dragon, the world of the "Thou shalts" and "Thou shalt nots." Certainly, part of what Nietzsche had in mind are the famous biblical "Thou shalts" and "Thou shalt nots"—the ten commandments—which essentially legislate how we are to live morally and ethically in the world. Thus, we also have to learn in this first stage how to come to grips with religion, because religion in some sense is unavoidable here, whether or not one believes in a particular theology. Formal religion, incidentally, is another aspect of the "Thou shalts" and "Thou shalt nots" that should never be confused with spirituality.

As we are growing up, we do not realize that we are really living in a desert, shouldering the burdens of the camel. It is only when we can sincerely say that there must be another way—something beyond this dragon, beyond just being a good boy and girl—that our spiritual needs begin to develop and grow. We realize there has to be something else that is meaningful, because what we thought was meaningful no longer seems so. It is at this point that *A Course in Miracles* enters. Both the workbook and the text are filled with reminders that the world is not our home. The very important Lesson 133, "I will not value what is valueless," helps us understand that everything we have valued is really valueless. The relationships, vocation, and financial security we possess or lack, the body we have or would like to have, above all our personal self—are all ultimately valueless.

This is the stage when the camel becomes transformed into the lion, who now wants to "conquer his freedom" and be master of his own destiny. We have progressed through the stage of humility. We have learned everything the world can teach us and now realize this is not what we want: we truly desire to be free and be our own master, not a slave to the masters of the world. We have come to understand that we cannot trust or believe anything the world tells us since it lies, being the effect of the ego's lie. In fact, in *A Course in Miracles* Jesus tells us that perception should not be believed (e.g., T-22.III). After all, why ask the one thing in all the universe that does not know, to tell us what reality is (T-20.III.7:5-7)? Why ask people to give words of wisdom when they are not wise themselves? Why ask the great brains of the world—*not the minds*—to tell us what is valuable, important, and how to find happiness here? We have spent the first half of our life doing just that, reading the great books, listening to smart people trying to make sense out of living here. Now we realize that none of this matters, for it does not give us the peace of God, the peace that transcends everything and can be affected by nothing.

In the first stage as a camel we have said yes to the world: "Yes, you will meet my needs and I will learn from you what will satisfy me." We begin of course by learning from our parents, and after a while we realize they are not perfect. We learn from our teachers, from other people in our families, from political, social, and religious leaders, and begin to see that what they said was perhaps true for a while, or it worked for us then—but it does not take us far enough. Thus, where before we said yes, now we say no. We realize that we have to look at the "Thou shalt" scales on the dragon and say this is not what we want. This is comparable to the important statement in the text where Jesus says that "'yes' means 'not no'" (T-21.VII.12:4). We look at the world, which is the negation of the truth, and say: "No, I do not want this anymore." In the first stage, we said yes to the negation of truth because we thought it *was* the truth. We thought the world worked the way it—the physicists, chemists, biologists, political scientists, theologians, psychologists, philosophers, and historians—told us it worked. Thinking that this was how the world operated, we said: "Yes, teach me." And so we learned and learned, but at some point we realized the world does not make sense. People lie, though not necessarily in a willful manner, but because *they do not know*. Why, again, should we listen to them?

The opposite of knowledge is not perception, for what is "all-encompassing can have no opposite" (T-in.1:8; italics omitted). Yet we can characterize the world of perception as ignorance or the lack of knowledge. The great Gnostic teachers taught this. *Gnosis* is the Greek word for "knowledge," and those who did not have the experience of gnosis (reality or truth) were the ones who did not know. Ignorance is truly the source of suffering and pain, the mother of all illusions. Again, those who lie to us—i.e., everyone—may not be deliberately concealing the truth; they simply do not know. How, then, can we be taught to awaken from the dream when everything we have read and been taught makes the dream real? How can we be taught, as Zarathustra was teaching, to laugh at the world when everyone thinks this world is real and

4. Stage Two: The Lion

what occurs here is tragic? Therefore, we must learn from someone who teaches a thought system that is outside the system, above the battleground, and thus does not believe that the cloud is a thundercloud, but rather sees it as the Course describes it—a flimsy veil that has no power to keep the light from shining through (T-18.IX.5-8). This is the burden of becoming a lion.

Who is the great dragon whom the spirit will no longer call lord and god? "Thou shalt" is the name of the great dragon. But the spirit of the lion says, "I will."

This is an expression of Nietzsche's concept of the *will to power*: "I will not be bound by the world. I will not take my cues from what the world tells me is truth and reality. I will not believe what I am told, whether it is from the news media or what people tell me— *unless they know.*" In time we can discern those who know, and they are the ones to whom we will listen. I have always liked the statement, told to me long ago by a wise man, the original source of which I cannot find: "When a wise man offers you poison, drink it; when a fool offers you an antidote, spurn it." It is the *content* of the wise that will heal and save us, and the *content* of the fool that will destroy us. Once again, why ask the one thing in all the universe that does not know, to tell us the truth? The only ones to listen to are those not taken in by the dream, for they will not simply help us live better within it. The camel seeks only the dream, but we come to recognize that this first stage will help us ultimately achieve the goal of awakening from it.

We therefore do not want to live in the desert. Jesus told Helen in the early weeks of the scribing:

The thing to do with the desert is to *leave.**

The camel takes us into the desert, except we do not yet know it is a desert. It is only when we are there that we realize it is nothing. The experience as a camel was not a waste, however, because we do not get to see the other side until we are first in the desert. Then we can look at what we have been taught and learned, and pronounce it as not true. Rather than being told what we should do, believe, or become, we now say, simply, "I will," which means we now choose our destiny. This is the *will to power.* To repeat:

But the spirit of the lion says, "I will." "Thou shalt" lies in his way, sparkling like gold ....

Think of the picture frame that Jesus describes in "The Two Pictures" (T-17.IV). The ego's picture is

---

* See my *Absence from Felicity: The Story of Helen Schucman and Her Scribing of A Course in Miracles*, p. 236.

death, its "kind" offering to us, adorned in a gorgeous, ornamented frame glittering with diamonds and rubies that conceals the picture. The frame of adornments is the dragon's scales, and it sparkles like a treasure, but in reality it is

...an animal covered with scales; and on every scale shines a golden "thou shalt."

This is the golden gleam of the ego, the seduction of specialness within which the world entraps us. It is a difficult stage because we now have to say that *everything* we have learned and have become is not true. The major challenge of this transition is to be able to exert this *will to power* without anger or attack, without seeking to destroy the world or ourselves, all the while recognizing that we cannot get to where we wish to go without first coming here. We then feel grateful for what we have become and have taught ourselves, because this will be the means that our teacher Jesus will use to help us move beyond our world to his.

We cannot go from the stage of being a camel to becoming a child without first identifying with the lion. To repeat, the lion says, "not no." It looks at the "Thou shalts," which are really the negation of love and truth, and says, "I do not want this anymore." Thus is the dragon killed, a major symbol in mythology, incidentally. The dragon symbolizes the ego, and the challenge, to restate it, is not to kill the dragon, because if we fight against the "Thou shalts" we will have made them real and they will return with a vengeance, literally. We simply recognize the ego for the illusion it is and then it will

> fade into [its own] nothingness from which it came (M-13.1:2).

However, Nietzsche was not speaking of this, and this is where *A Course in Miracles* helps us complete the journey. In the text, Jesus teaches that the disappearance of the body is simply a "quiet melting in" (T-18.VI.14:6); there is no struggle against it, no destruction. The body merely dissolves into the illusory mind where it has always been; and the thoughts of hate, guilt, and fear are replaced by love. The body might physically remain as other eyes see it, but as an independent entity it will simply disappear. And so we do not fight against the dragon, but with Jesus' eyes as our vision, we look with open eyes at what it is. We understand that the dragon is not society or the laws of religion. It is only a projection of our own need to remain separate. Recall:

> Call it [the original error] not sin.... Invest it not with guilt.... And above all, *be not afraid of it* (T-18.I.6:7-9).

If we fight against the ego we do exactly what Jesus asks us *not* to do: take the illusion seriously and make it real. Still, we must look at it, and so be able to say and mean that the world we made holds nothing that we want (W-pI.128).

To make this important point again, we need to realize that we do not reject, as wasted, the first half of our life, for everything we have experienced has led us to the point where we are now willing to say that there must be something else. This is critical; otherwise we will be too hard on ourselves. Remember, this course begins where our life in the world ends: with our successes (or failures). We have managed to learn how to survive in the world, and we begin to embrace *A Course in Miracles* when we recognize that we are not happy; that, to quote Helen and Bill, "there must be another way." Indeed, the Course would not have come through Helen until she and Bill had reached the dead end of recognizing that nothing here really worked. They both had achieved success in the world, being highly regarded professors in a prestigious academic-medical institution. Yet they had to look at themselves and realize that something was missing.

It is not helpful for us to look back on our lives and feel bad about them, since that only serves to negate our classroom of learning. We need to remember that we cannot be a lion that slays the dragon in the desert unless we first travel into the desert as a camel. We do not want to skip over steps. Again, the "Thou shalts" are very appealing, which is why Nietzsche calls them "gold." To those who identify with the world and want something from it, the world is a treasure to win; and we gain the treasures in the world, as we know, by killing off our rivals. As egos we triumph, whether over a school and faculty in order to complete our education, over a business in order to make money, or a relationship in order to seduce and manipulate the other person so that our needs are met. We all seek to slay the dragon of specialness. Yet this is not really the dragon Nietzsche is talking about, because seeking to slay the dragon *is* the dragon, so the dragon of specialness is never truly slain. In other words. as we have seen, striving to defeat the world, the embodiment of the thought of separation, merely reinforces its seeming reality. We thus never get to undo the real dragon, which is our mind's decision for the ego. To slay the dragon of specialness, therefore, is to look at the ego's thought system and gently say: "This is no longer the world I value, and so I can choose a better one."

Values, thousands of years old, shine on these scales; and thus speaks the mightiest of all dragons: "All value of all things shines on me. All value has long been created, and I am all created

value. Verily, there shall be no more 'I will.'"
Thus speaks the dragon.

The lion's "I will" is the greatest threat to the dragon, who says there will no longer be an "I will." There is no room for an individual asserting his *will to power* (not to be confused, to reinforce this clarification, with the ego's self-assertiveness). There is no room in the world (the kingdom of the dragons) for people who regain access to their decision-making minds in order to choose to remember who they really are. This spiritual power has to be destroyed, which is society's purpose. We often seek, for example, to punish the people who are different. Nietzsche was writing personally, since he himself experienced a great deal of rejection and criticism in his life, as did his alter ego Zarathustra. Remember that the dragon is the world's values, which are the projections in form of the central ego value: I exist—a separate entity, independent and autonomous of my Creator. This is *the* value, encompassing the value of protecting, cherishing, and preserving the self we believe we stole from Heaven. All worldly values reinforce this supreme value, and our purloined self is protected in the mind by projecting it into the world that is perceived as real, thereby making real the ego's dream of separation.

The core of what the world values is always the same, even though the specifics of what we hold dear differ from culture to culture and age to age. Some things we want because they give us pleasure, and others we avoid because they give us pain. However, all things—pleasurable and painful—make the body's dream real. The ego loves the idea of bettering or changing the world, which is one of the more seductive of the dragon's scales because it gives the dream a reality it cannot have. The mindless world denies the mind's power, the will of choosing to become the *overman* who transcends the world. It is not that we cease to exist as physical beings, but that we realize that the body is not who we are. We thus rise above the battleground of the value-laden scales of the dragon.

Again, the dragon says: "All value has long been created, and I am all created value. Verily, there shall be no more 'I will.' Thus speaks the dragon." This pits the individual against society. However, if we see the conflict only on that level, we will never get beyond it. Society is simply a projection of what we are really pitted against, which is the mind's *decision* to be an ego, to be in our wrong-minded instead of right-minded state, to remain in the dream of separation that culminates in life as a body, rather than to awaken from the nightmare of separation.

My brothers, why is there a need in the spirit for the lion? Why is not the beast of burden, which renounces and is reverent, enough?

Why do we have to go through this stage? Why is it not enough just to be obedient and reverent to the world, obeying its dragons? Here is the answer:

To create new values—that even the lion cannot do....

"To create new values" is the right-minded yes. The lion only says no, the "not no" that is the condition for the "sacred yes." This is why it is not enough to be a lion. If we are only a lion, we will never get to be a child and to embrace the new value that is our spiritual self. We cannot skip steps and become the child until we first become a lion, until we are able to look at the ego thought system and say: "I do not want this anymore."

Nietzsche is not only talking about an external rebellion against the inanities of the world, which he obviously felt were most inane, but about an inner process. This is where his so-called followers got off track. He was not preaching revolution, demagoguery, or Nazism, all of which he would have strenuously opposed. Rather, his focus was on our becoming who we really are as *spiritual beings*. If we only say no to the world, we will never become a child, because such

59

opposition is exactly what the dragon wants. We will kill that particular form of the dragon, and another will quickly rise to take its place. Nietzsche's point is realizing, which *A Course in Miracles* makes very clear, that the external dragons are mere projections of the inner dragons. The dragon we see is an outside picture of an inner wish, the wish to be an ego, which we then project onto the world (T-24.VII.8:8-10). This process of projection leads us to conclude that it is the world that does not allow us to be free— restricting, inhibiting, and obstructing our progress; keeping us unhappy, lonely, and miserable; and always lying to us. Therefore it is the world that has to be slain and overcome, for that is what we believe to be the problem.

This, then, is one way of understanding Nietzsche's idea of *eternal recurrence*: we go around and around and around the same problem of separation, and nothing ever changes. But it is important to see *why* nothing ever changes. Again, the dragon is merely a projection of what is inside. We believe the ego is a dragon, and the scale on that ego dragon says: "Thou shalt not look at me because, if you do, you will die." This is echoed in the Course's expression of the ego's counsel:

> Loudly the ego tells you not to look inward, for
> if you do your eyes will light on sin, and God

will strike you blind. This you believe, and so
you do not look (T-21.IV.2:3-4).

So we listen to the original "Thou shalt" and do not go
to the mind and look at the dragon; instead we go outside and see there the dragons, with whom we must do
battle in order to survive.

In other words, it is not enough to say that the
world we see holds nothing that we want (W-pI.128),
but we need also to affirm that there is another world
we do want (W-pI.129). We negate the lies of the
world, but only to make room for the truth within.
This was the same point Jesus made near the end of
the text in discussing the place of death to which all
the world's roads inevitably lead:

> The roads this world can offer seem to be quite
> large in number, but the time must come when
> everyone begins to see how like they are to one
> another.... All must reach this point, and go be-
> yond it. It is true indeed there is no choice at all
> within the world. But this is not the lesson in
> itself....
>
> Who would be willing to be turned away from
> all the roadways of the world, unless he under-
> stood their real futility? Is it not needful that he
> should begin with this, *to seek another way
> instead*? For while he sees a choice where there
> is none, what power of decision can he use? The
> great release of power must begin with learning

where it really has a use. And what decision has power if it be applied in situations without choice? (T-31.IV.3:3,7-9; 5; italics mine)

The *other way* is returning to the mind where meaningful choice is made, our gaining access to the mind's power of decision. It was our wrong-minded decision that, again, is the dragon that needs to be slain since it is the source of our experiences of being a slave to the dictates of others.

And so, to summarize, we are in the desert wanting another way, which means wanting another teacher. We thus choose Jesus, who helps us realize that the value of the external dragon—society giving us its "Thou shalts" and "Thou shalt nots"—is that it helps us realize that *we* are the dictator. We therefore need to work with the projected personification because that is how we go inside to slay the dragon that is the mind's mistaken choice.

To create new values—that even the lion cannot do; but the creation of freedom for oneself for new creation—that is within the power of the lion.

In other words, while the lion can assert the power of the mind's will, it is the child that finally makes the right choice. But the lion is able to say: "I will. I have a mind; this is my decision. I do not have to be bound by the dragons and the scales of 'Thou shalt'." We can now realize, as the Course says near the end of Chapter 27, that we are the dreamers of the dream; we are no longer victims of the world's dream, unless we choose to see ourselves that way (T-27.VII,VIII). Our reality is outside the dream, and as the dream's dreamer, we are not bound by the "Thou shalts" of the dragon, by what other people do, say, or seem to make us feel. To paraphrase from the text: "Let the dragons be as hateful and as vicious as they may, they could have no effect on us unless we failed to recognize they are our dragons" (T-27.VIII.10:6). The dragons of our world are certainly malevolently vicious, hateful, and cruel, and, moreover, they enjoy people's suffering. All this is true but, to repeat, the world's dragons can affect us only when we forget that we are the ones responsible for our reactions of hurt, pain, and anger. The lion, in other words, recognizes that the dragons are his dream, and accepts responsibility for what he feels.

Nietzsche is telling us that the lion cannot create the new values; that remains for the next stage when the spirit (i.e., the mind) chooses the innocence of the child. The lion can look at the sin and guilt that is projected outside and recognize it is really within, and that he has the power to choose against it. This is the "I will," the assertion of the mind's power to choose. Once again, one can see how corrupted that

63

idea became in its use as a rationale for Nazism or any totalitarian regime; a gross distortion of the mind's power to exercise its freedom and choose a new creation. *This* the lion can do. As Jesus says in his course:

> The power of decision is your one remaining freedom as a prisoner of this world (T-12.VII.9:1).

Such freedom is Nietzsche's whole point. The lion does not choose innocence, but realizes that it has a choice between innocence and guilt. It made itself into the great dragon, and can just as easily choose against it.

To reiterate, the first stage is placing ourselves humbly under the laws of the world. This stage cannot be avoided. This is why when we made our collective and individual dreams, we made ourselves the way we are, necessitating this learning. We therefore need to go successfully through the normal (to the species) developmental stages. They are denied or ignored at our own peril, in the sense that if we do not practice our daily lessons of forgiveness, we will never reach our goal. True spiritual attainment is the final stage, but we will not arrive there without our having more or less successfully navigated our way through the earlier stages. Otherwise we will have subverted our spiritual journey.

Here is what the power of the lion entails:

The creation of freedom for oneself and a sacred "No" even to duty—for that, my brothers, the lion is needed.

We no longer feel bound by what the world tells us to do. This does not mean nihilism, that we break laws or do nothing, but, to make this point once again, it refers to an *inner* freedom from the world's laws. Guilt, attack, and suffering are the harsh laws of the ego's world of separation and specialness. To this we say the "sacred no," which is the meaning of the lesson, "I am under no laws but God's" (W-pI.76), and Jesus' words from the text:

> Salvation is no more than a reminder this world is not your home. Its laws are not imposed on you, its values are not yours (T-25.VI.6:1-2).

Beforehand, the world demanded our loyalty to its thought system of specialness, attack, and suffering —all forms of its dictum of separate interests. This is what we said yes to. Now we are being asked, as a lion, to look at all that and say: "No, I no longer want that." The yes to this world of the ego was a negation of love and truth. With Jesus beside us, we now look at that negation and say no to it—"not no." Earlier in the text, Jesus makes the same point using other words as he explains that the responsibility of the miracle worker is *"to deny the denial of truth"* (T-12.II.1:5). The lion looks at the denial of truth, at what he said yes to—everything the world holds dear, which boils down to the doctrine of separate interests (*one or the other*)—and says: "I do not want to do this anymore. Everything I had valued before is value-less." What the world defined as yes and as truth, was really its denial. Again, this is not about anything external. I cannot emphasize this enough. If we do not realize that this is not about the world or the body, we may find ourselves doing hostile things to ourselves and others, thinking they are kind and loving. What needs to be changed is a *thought system*. The behavior inevitably follows.

In the section in the teacher's manual that addresses the issue of external changes, "Are Changes Required in the Life Situations of God's Teachers?" (M-9), Jesus explains that external shifts are not the emphasis. What is truly important is a *change in attitude*. Then, as he further states, the fundamental change that is required of all God's teachers is the *giving up of judgment*. This would free our minds of any ego thoughts that would contaminate our judgments about behavior. Our focus thus shifts from the external world of bodies to the internal world of the mind's decision-making power and, more specifically, to which teacher we wish to learn from: the teacher of judgment and attack, or the teacher of forgiveness and peace.

All the world's laws, rules, regulations, and prejudices are projections in form of the same ego thoughts that seem to imprison us. They basically say: "Thou shalt not question the ego. Thou shalt not look at the ego." But the lion looks, and where before it saw an opaque thundercloud, it now sees a flimsy veil with no power to conceal the light—what it means to be the *overman*. We transcend not only the world, but our own species as well. We become more than a member of homo sapiens because we realize that the Sonship of God is *content*, not form. We therefore recognize our unity with everything, expressing the Buddha's compassionate nature, and cannot be cruel to anyone or anything. For who can feel the Love of God within and be hostile to another person, animal, plant, or even a machine (like a car or computer when they malfunction)? An inner gentleness and kindness extends through us and embraces everyone and everything, regardless of their form. This is the inevitable result of becoming a lion who has looked at what the world and ego say yes to, understands it as a no, a negation of truth, and simply says: "I do not want this. I choose differently."

To assume the right to new values—that is the most terrifying assumption for a reverent spirit that would bear much.

Nietzsche keeps returning to the image of the spirit bearing much. He is telling us this is a difficult path. There are burdens, but they are not externally imposed. Ultimately, these are our own fears and resistance to the truth. Nietzsche never used the term *resistance* the way Freud did, but he was well aware of its meaning. One can see this defense at work throughout the book in people's responses to Zarathustra. They do not want to hear the truth, which is why Nietzsche subtitled his *opus*, "A Book for All and None." Jesus could just as easily have done the same thing with *A Course in Miracles*. They are books for *all* because they comprise a universal teaching, and yet they are books for *none* because no one wants to hear the truth. No one knew this better than Nietzsche.

Our fear of the truth, therefore, gives rise to our resistance, and that was the source of the great trepidation with which Nietzsche approached, even within himself, the idea of *eternal recurrence*. As we have already seen, this notion bordered on the understanding that linear time is an illusion. Remember, this was before Einstein and quantum physics. Nietzsche had an intuitive understanding that the world is not what we think it is. Its movement through time is circular, as we keep recirculating the same experiences over and over again. Nietzsche did not know the ultimate answer, but he certainly knew what the world was, just as Freud did, who also did not know the ultimate answer, but well understood how the ego functioned. They were kindred spirits.

In light of this, it is interesting to note that in the context of his little gem, Nietzsche spent a relatively small amount of time on the child. The greater bulk of "On the Three Metamorphoses" discusses the camel and the lion. This is, in part, because there is very little one can say about truth. More personally, however, Nietzsche did not know the child as intuitively as he knew the camel and lion. He lived the life of a camel in the first part of his life, and then for the rest of it he was a lion who taught that all values are wrong, for the world lies, Christianity distorts the truth, people sell out, becoming part of the system instead of transcending it. Even his once-loved Wagner sold out, he felt.

What Nietzsche taught, through Zarathustra, is the *overman*, the one who transcends himself and moves beyond who he is. This, as we have seen, would be roughly equivalent to what Jesus refers to as the advanced teacher of God, the last step before attaining the real world. "To assume the right to new values—that is the most terrifying assumption…." Why?

Because our life—the very fabric of our existence, its DNA, if you will—is based on the value of separation, of being separate from our Source, possessing a separate identity that keeps us separate from each other. We are terrified to say this value is wrong, for we fear the new value. But the lion does not know what this is. That awareness belongs to the child.

Verily, to him it is preying, and a matter for a beast of prey.

The lion preys on the old values. Nietzsche uses the symbol of the lion because it is the beast of prey, the king of all beasts that is more powerful than the others and defeats them. Yet, as we have seen, Nietzsche is not speaking about brute force, militarism, or triumphing over evildoers. If there were bombs in his time, he would not be talking about dropping them on other people. The *overman* possesses the *inner* power that preys on the ego and devours it, not as an act of aggression, but as the aforementioned "quiet melting in" (see p. 54 above).

He once loved "thou shalt" as most sacred...

This is the lion when it was a camel, the spirit (i.e., mind or soul) beginning its journey. It is difficult in the first decades of life not to embrace the world's values. We would not pursue them if we did not at least on some level embrace our various special relationships:

family, romance, bodily pleasure, education, vocation, money, or having an attractive body—all these
we revered and held sacred. I cannot emphasize this
enough: we do not reach the latter part of the journey
until we first go through this part. Before we can
choose *against* the world, we first have to feel comfortable *in* the world. Otherwise we will be handi-
capped throughout our life, and will never become a
child. Indeed, we will be the child in the sense that
Jesus talks about it in *A Course in Miracles*: one who
knows nothing, and is always throwing temper tantrums, demanding attention, and justifying feelings of
being unfairly treated.

**He once loved "thou shalt" as most sacred: now he
must find illusion and caprice even in the most
sacred, that freedom from his love may become
his prey: the lion is needed for such prey.**

We need to become free of what we once loved,
which we do by choosing against it, even letting go of
what we believed was the most sacred object of our
identification—our individual, special self. We realize that this was all mere "illusion and caprice." Yet
our fear is great, which is why achieving this stage is
so difficult.

Of the six stages discussed in "Development of
Trust" (M-4.I.A), the lion essentially encompasses the

first four, as stated earlier. The first three are essentially the same, as they lead us from the external and bring us within, focusing on the realization that what we heretofore had judged as valuable is now valueless. This is from the second stage:

(M-4.I.4:3-4) He will find that many, if not most of the things he valued before will merely hinder his ability to transfer what he has learned to new situations as they arise. Because he has valued what is really valueless, he will not generalize the lesson for fear of loss and sacrifice.

The fear is that we will lose ourselves if we generalize what we are learning. Thus, not only does a particular thing we had valued no longer have value for us, but *nothing* here holds any value. We recognize the inherent valuelessness of everything in the world, and that is what terrifies us so. This reflects the transfer of training (or generalization) Jesus discusses at the beginning of the workbook (W-in.4-7). Now we begin to realize that it is not the things of the world that are valueless, it is the thing in ourselves— *what we think we are*—that is truly valueless. The world is simply a projection of the nothingness of our ego self. Realizing this fact engenders the terror to which Nietzsche refers.

(5:5) Therefore, the period of overlap is apt to be one in which the teacher of God feels called upon to sacrifice his own best interests on behalf of truth.

This is the problem. The ego tells us that if we relinquish the values of the world for this new value (the child's innocence), we will disappear; losing ourselves by sacrificing our "best interests." Quite simply, these interests ensure the survival of our separate and special identity, yet someone else is held responsible for it, deserving the punishment we secretly believe should be ours. This, then, is our twofold value for the world: preserving our separated selves and blaming another for our misery. Consequently we can see why we love to hate and inflict pain on others, whether in the guise of national interests that justify torturing the enemy, or in the personal world of special relationships. Inflicting pain upholds the ego's primary value. My hurting you comes because you deserve it. You are second class and I am first class; you do not count, for all that matters is *my* race, *my* religion, *my* country, *my* self. Thus do we uphold the value of personal existence, but at another's expense—the ego's kingdom of heaven on earth.

We can therefore see why we would flee from forgiveness as a way of life; it undermines adherence to our basic value. It highlights all that is wrong with the world. And so, for example, it is not this government's policy versus another's that is the issue. *All* policies are hateful because they are based on nationalism and separate interests. The only true value in this world, because it reflects Heaven's value of perfect Oneness, is shared interests—a purpose shared by *all* people. If I am faithful to that value, however, I give up who I am, the very substance of myself, the foundation of my special existence. This is why the first three stages in "Development of Trust" are described as painful and, in fact, are terrifying. Indeed, some of the words Jesus uses to describe them are: *undoing, painful, difficult, distress, enormous conflict*, which is why becoming a lion is not easy.

Yet if we behave like ferocious lions, flailing wildly at everything that is wrong in our personal or collective worlds, we are not lions at all, but simply camels masquerading as what we are not. What could be sillier than a camel saying it is a lion! But this is what we do. Remember that the camel adheres to and upholds the values of the world. Fighting against these values merely reinforces one's belief in them. Whether we are subservient to something or fight against it, we make it real and as a result can never be free of it. Love therefore is absent, because love in this world is the awareness of our shared need of forgiveness, and thus is the absence of all separation, separate interests, and opposition.

(5:6-7) He has not realized as yet how wholly impossible such a demand would be. He can learn this only as he actually does give up the valueless.

We need to recognize the absolute insanity of believing that to compromise our happiness, and therefore lose, is the inevitable effect of choosing the truth; sanity is realizing that our best interests will suffer when we identify with the core value of the ego's illusory thought system of separation and hate, which is inherently valueless.

(5:8) Through this, he learns that where he anticipated grief, he finds a happy lightheartedness instead ....

This describes Zarathustra at his best. Throughout his journey he laughs and dances, reflecting the "happy lightheartedness" that comes when we elevate above the clouds, looking down to see not thunderclouds but flimsy wisps of nothing that cannot prevent the light from shining through. The lightheartedness Jesus describes, the basis of love in this world, is the essence of Nietzsche's Zarathustra. It is what makes us all happy learners (T-14.II).

(5:8) ...where he thought something was asked of him, he finds a gift bestowed on him.

This is the heart of what Jesus means at the beginning of Chapter 24 in the text:

> To learn this course requires willingness to question every value that you hold. Not one can be kept hidden and obscure but it will jeopardize your learning (T-24.in.2:1-2).

This means *every* value—all the "Thou shalts" and "Thou shalt nots" that comprise the dragon's multitudinous scales. At some point we will generalize this teaching and realize that the dragon does not have thousands of scales, but only one. We will come to understand that the values and concepts the world told us were true—religious, political, economic, social— were false, made to uphold the ultimate value of our special existence as a self separate from Self. This specialness is the dragon's scale.

This is why Jesus says, as does Zarathustra, that we must question every value. This is what it means to slay the dragon. We begin by questioning the externals—what our parents, religions, political leaders, or any authority has told us. We question everything. The ancient mystery school of the Rosicrucians taught that our lives must be a walking question mark. At first we learn from everyone and everything—the humility of

4. Stage Two: The Lion

the camel—for this is how we grow. At some point, when we reach maturity in terms of living in the world, we start the questioning process and thus become lions. We look at the world's values, the "sacred yeses" that govern life here, and see that these were really negations of the truth. We look and say: "*I* have been the negation of the truth and no longer choose to be this. I can no longer blame the world, for I indeed am my own master."

We are now led to what Jesus refers to as the fourth stage in the development of trust, the stage of peace, when we realize we cannot be affected by the world. No matter what happens, we no longer value what the world values, but only what is truly valuable in us. This becomes, operationally speaking, our relationship with the Holy Spirit or Jesus, or any other presence that symbolizes our non-ego self. Whenever we become upset, we go to our minds and say, as Lesson 34 teaches: "I could see peace instead of this" or "I could see Jesus instead of this; I could be *with* Jesus instead of with my ego; I could feel his love and his peace instead of what I am feeling now." This shift is our new value, and is the gift bestowed on us. It is not the ultimate value, because we are still in stage four, the stage of the lion and individuality. However, we realize that what is truly valuable is not the external. Nothing outside can mean anything because it is not the peace of God, nor is it the love that embraces all people. Again, whatever thought that does not embrace everyone, *without exception*, is valueless. This is one of the most central criteria in distinguishing between what is valuable and what is valueless. If a thought makes differences among the Sonship significant, it is worthless. If it embraces 99.99 percent of the population, but excludes a mere fraction, it is still worthless. The Sonship of God is total, a perfect whole; and each of us is an integral part of that whole.

The world's different values all come down to the one the world holds most dear: the principle of *one or the other*—someone wins, another loses, and I am going to make certain that I am the winner. Even if I appear to be losing, in the end I will win, for my loss means that someone has done this to me; someone has victimized, persecuted, tortured, betrayed, or abandoned me. And so in the end, God will lift *me* up and cast everyone else down into hell. This is the insanity the world values above all else.

Being a lion thus means looking at everything the world holds as valuable—there is a winner and a loser—and saying we no longer want that. This state, comparable to the fourth stage in the development of trust, leads to peace and a sense of freedom; we can now be happy and peaceful no matter what is going on

4. Stage Two: The Lion

around us. This allows us to accept the *will to power* that was sacred to Nietzsche, which says: "I will. I am the all-powerful dreamer of my dreams, not a weak and vulnerable dream figure who is 'at the mercy of things beyond [him], forces [he] cannot control, and thoughts that come to [him] against [his] will (T-19.IV-D.7:4).'"

Recall this passage:

> Let them be as hateful and as vicious as they may, they could have no effect on you unless you failed to recognize it is your dream (T-27.VIII.10:6).

Imagine the real power this gives us. We now truly have all power in Heaven and earth, as the gospels describe Jesus as having (e.g., Matthew 28:18), which is why the Course cites that passage several times (e.g., T-5.II.9:2, W-pI.191.9:1). As decision-making minds, we have the power to choose the ego's hell or the Holy Spirit's Heaven. No one can do this for us. No one can drive us to hell or lead us to Heaven. We alone have this power, the will of our minds to choose. This choice is not the end of the story, but it does get us out of the desert. We are now free of the dragon because we realize that the "Thou shalts" were only our decision, a decision we now happily correct. Therefore, questioning our commitment to the world's values—a relationship, a job, the way we view illness, politics, economics, or the world in general—reflects a more fundamental change of mind.

Before we discuss some passages from the workbook that are relevant to this stage of the lion, let us review how we arrived here.

Summary

The framework for our discussion has been the spiritual journey, a journey that begins in what appears to be a very non-spiritual place: learning how to live in the world and adjust to it. We embrace worldly values only so that when we reach middle age and are reasonably mature—whatever our chronological age—we can understand that the world does not make sense, and lacks all value because it does not give us the peace of God. If something does not lead us to the peace of God, the only true value, how could it possibly be of any value to us?

The first stage, what Nietzsche refers to as the camel, consists of humbly assuming the burden of being in the world, physically and psychologically mastering the art of survival. This is no mean feat. We do not have to live perfectly, but we need to live with sincerity. A Hindu tradition holds that a man raises and supports his family, and when the children are grown, leaves to pursue his spiritual path. I am not sure where that leaves his wife, but that is another issue. In a sense, this tradition is referring to the camel—that we master living in the world as we develop a sense of self. And then we move on. Thus, as camels, we say yes to the world, believing that it is meaningful and will bring us what we want, only to step back, look at our lives, and then say that we no longer desire its gifts.

The second metamorphosis occurs when we finally open our eyes and realize we are in a desert in which nothing grows, and that there is no hope of anything meaningful occurring here. We thereby declare that there must be another way, another teacher, or another symbol we can relate to. At this point, then, our self (or spirit) is transformed into a lion. What heretofore had been valued is now seen to be valueless. Again, and most importantly, this second stage will make no sense unless we have gone through the first stage.

The questioning of values, which occurs in the mind, can come in different forms. It does not necessarily involve changing our behavior or roles, as we have seen. It does not mean that we walk out on a job, or abandon our vocation and family. This transformation of values might begin by questioning what we are hearing from elected public officials, the news media, or what we listen to in a synagogue on Saturday or church on Sunday. The same words we have been hearing for years no longer ring true. We question our primary relationships—indeed, all relationships—seeing how they were built on bargains of specialness. We begin to realize that something is rotten in the state of our household or business, and increasingly become aware of the specialness values we had embraced, not seeing the ego thought system lurking behind what we thought of as love or duty. Therefore, these relationships were not truly loving or happy making; instead they were vehicles to maintain the judgments that anchored us still further in the world of illusion.

And so we question, beginning with whatever level we find comfortable. What is important is that we realize that in questioning something external—a relationship or job, our views on illness, politics, economics, etc.—we are but reflecting our mind's decision. If we do not bring what we are experiencing back within, we will not be able to learn and practice what Jesus is teaching us in his course. To be sure, we have to pay attention to our experiences in the world as bodies, but only insofar as they lead us to what is going on in our minds:

> The world you see is... the outside picture of an inward condition (T-21.in.1:2,5).

This is why it is so important to remember that the special relationship is not truly between us and another, but always between our decision maker and the ego; similarly, the holy relationship occurs only when our decision maker has chosen Jesus as its teacher. What we experience as a special or holy relationship between bodies is simply a projection in form of a decision we made to be wrong- or right-minded. There is therefore only one special relationship and one holy relationship. Again, all external relationships—body to body—are merely projections (from the ego) or reflections (from the Holy Spirit) of the mind's choice. As we begin to question the value of a relationship, we become aware of the bargains we have made with others, whether it be personal or work-related relationships, or ones existing in our imagination between ourselves and public officials. The good news is that the fact that we question a relationship is already saying that we are looking with open eyes at the value we had placed on the mind's relationship with the ego.

We can now understand that before Helen and Bill had their fateful encounter that concluded with their agreeing to find "another way," they both had made a decision in their minds to set aside their ego and not value its offerings of conflict, anger, judgment, and misery. This decision expressed itself in terms of their discussion, because Helen and Bill believed they were bodies having a relationship with each other. However, their being able to shift their purpose and join together to find the other way was the result of their having first made the choice within. Once again, we see the external as the means of returning to the internal. Revisiting a passage that is parallel to what was quoted above, we read that perception

> is the outward picture of a wish; an image that you wanted to be true (T-24.VII.8:10).

We need to be aware of our experiences in the world, as lions, and recognize that the world is not what we thought. Becoming financial successes, having rewarding relationships, or raising families has not brought us the peace of God. The willingness to question values is the effect of the underlying cause of questioning the value of the ego itself. As camels, we do not know we have a mind, for we still experience ourselves as bodies dealing with other bodies and coping with life in the world. Since we are unaware of the mind, our willingness to question what is outside opens the door that allows our decision makers to say that there must be another way of looking. As quickly as we can, and *A Course in Miracles* tells us that the miracle's purpose is to save us time (e.g., T-1.II.6), we need to realize that changing our perception of another mirrors the changing of our self-perception: "I am no longer a child of guilt, but a child of God."

This enables us to generalize. If we are always having to shift perceptions of every relationship, our various work situations, or world events, we will never be healed because the specifics are almost infinite. With over six billion people in the world, and millions of other species, not to mention ever-changing life circumstances, there are multitudinous objects for our projections. However, if we bring every perception back to its common source—our choosing to be in the wrong mind with the ego or the right mind with Jesus—then everything will change. Generalizing, we recognize that all misperceptions (the wrong mind's interpretations of the external world) come from the mind's single mistaken choice, and thus we learn that our worldly experience can be shifted by undoing the original error of choosing the wrong teacher.

The workbook lesson "I am under no laws but God's" extends our discussion of this second stage of spiritual development.

"I am under no laws but God's"

In many places in *A Course in Miracles* we find Jesus asking us to begin the process of becoming lions and question what heretofore we had held to be sacrosanct—the different forms of specialness; the ways we have related to our bodies and those of others.

Nowhere is this more clearly stated than in Lesson 76, where Jesus enumerates the various "laws" that govern our lives and that we obviously value. And so, for example, we value the laws of medicine that we believe help us feel better, while the laws of sickness bring pain and suffering; the laws of special relationships hold that we will be happy if people meet our special needs, and the laws of money teach that we will be better off with an abundance of "paper strips" and "metal discs" (T-27.VIII.2:2; also, see below W-pI.76.3:2). In this lesson, Jesus asks us to consider these worldly values very specifically.

(1:1) We have observed before how many sense-less things have seemed to you to be salvation.

These are the various things in the world that, as camels, we learn to do so that we will feel good. Thus, if I study hard in school and graduate I will get a better job; if I get a better job I will earn a higher salary; and if I also feel fulfilled in my work, I will be happier still. This is salvation in the world's eyes, and essentially consists of achieving certain goals: relationships, families, and bodies that look or feel as we want them to. We embrace these values at first, and actually need to if we are to survive. Yet when we realize that we want more than mere survival, we move to the next stage when we, as lions, begin to question our lives. This lesson helps us do just that.

(1:2-3) Each has imprisoned you with laws as senseless as itself. You are not bound by them.

As bodies we *are* bound by these laws. Indeed, the only way we would not be bound is to realize we are not a body, to lift ourselves above the battleground, elevating ourselves as did Zarathustra. As minds we are not bound by the world below the clouds of separation and guilt. This does not mean, however, that we deny the body and its needs, which is why, to repeat, the first stage of our life is so important. We are taught as lions to deny only the value we have given the body, which is to root us in the dream, thus preventing return to the dream's *cause*: the mind's decision for the ego. Valuing the body ensures that we will never direct our minds away from the dream and return home, which, needless to say, is the fundamental ego strategy of keeping us forever mindless.

Valuing anything in this world is a way of keeping us here. The value is intentional and purposive. The incredible thing is that we *want* to believe the lie, and that is because we are children of the lie, the original untruth being that we separated from our Source. Everything that comes from that ontological illusion shares in it. One need only think of the fact that we know that politicians lie, but that does not stop us from believing them. This has nothing to do with party affiliation, our principles, or whether we like the way a candidate looks. It has to do only with the more fundamental value that *we want to make the lie real*, for this keeps our separated and special identity real.

It is truly terrifying for us to say that we do not believe anything that anyone says, yet that would be the wisest thing we could say, as Socrates taught over twenty-five hundred years ago. Recall this line from near the end of the text:

> There is no statement that the world is more afraid to hear than this:
>
> > *I do not know the thing I am, and therefore do not know what I am doing, where I am, or how to look upon the world or on myself.*
>
> Yet in this learning is salvation born. And What you are will tell you of Itself (T-31.V.17:6-9).

Since everyone born into the world is the projected product of the original lie, we all must lie. Even taking a breath bespeaks the reality of the ego's dream of separation and the world's dream of bodies that are born, live, and die. A fundamental principle in *A Course in Miracles* is that *ideas leave not their source*. If the source is a lie, then every idea that comes from it must also be a lie, including its projections. Thus we read in the workbook:

> The world was made as an attack on God.... The world was meant to be a place where God could enter not, and where His Son could be apart from Him (W-pII.3.2:1,4).

Given the intrinsic attack thought that *is* the world, why should we believe anything we are taught here? If God is not here, and God is Love and truth, then who in their right minds would ever want what the world offers? Yet since we all do, and clearly have chosen to be here, we are all perforce in our wrong minds.

This, then, is what we need to look at and understand why we value the lie and choose to believe in illusions when something in us knows better. It is a fact of human existence that we are only interested in *me, myself, and I*: our separate selves and individual interests. We all want our special needs met, and we deceive others to get what we want by denying the essential oneness of reality, reflected in the world by the sameness of mind that unites us all. While one might discern degrees of lies in our differentiated world, the bottom line remains that our merely identifying with the body's laws of birth, life, and death, impossible to deny once we believe we are here, is itself a lie. Within the illusion, on the other hand, the truth is that we are minds outside time and space. From the acceptance of our identities as split minds, we are made ready to awaken to the truth of our reality as extensions of the One Mind.

The lion understands that we are not defined by the body and the world, and that is why he destroys the dragon and its scales. Once again, though, this destruction is not done with a sword or through worldly power, but simply by looking at the ego with a gentle smile—Zarathustra's laughing and dancing. We laugh and dance around the dragon and it disappears. In *The Magic Flute*, Mozart's penultimate and most wonderful opera, there is the enchanting scene where the hero, Tamino, finds himself in the midst of threatening animals. To deal with his fear, he begins to play his magic flute. The animals start dancing and proceed to lie down. This is what we are to do with the ego's dragon. We take out our magic flute of forgiveness and play it. In the face of its kind and gentle music the ego's dragon becomes a little puppy. This ferocious animal ends up as a little mouse, to shift metaphors, tucked away in the corner of the universe, screaming its lungs out with no one to hear (T-22.V.4). Therefore, we do not fight the ego; we only forgive it for the monster it never was.

In other words, what binds us to the world is not the world; it is *our need to be a part of the world*, part of the lie. There is an indisputable litmus test for discerning whether something is a lie: If someone says, does, or values anything that does not embrace the *entire* Sonship in its shared interests, it is a lie. It was once said of Henry Kissinger that you know he is lying when his lips move. Yet that is true not only of the former Secretary of State; we all lie. After all, we move our lips and mouths when we breathe. And so, we need to spend our lives practicing this simple principle of shared versus separate interests; recognizing that failing to include *everyone* in the Sonship is to exclude everyone. In applying this principle we will never go wrong.

Therefore we can say that the fundamental law of this world, on which rest all the others stated in this lesson, is the law of separate interests. The belief that we had an interest separate from God's is what began the ego and the physical universe. This is how we can tell whether we are truly being a lion on the way to becoming a child, or still desiring to be a camel that only looks like a lion or a child. In other words, the question uppermost in our minds should be: Do I really want to leave the thought system that made this world, or do I want to become even more firmly rooted in it? Unfortunately, formal religions and spiritual paths have been used as weapons against true religion and spirituality, making it seem as if they are helping us leave the world and the thought system of separation that underlies it, when all they really do is anchor us more securely to it. Again, the sign that a teaching, regardless of its form, is false is that it does not embrace all people *without exception*; it does not lead us past the forms, which inevitably separate and differentiate, to the content of love that unifies us.

Thus, the laws that this lesson lists are simply expressions in form of the basic law that says separate interests is the truth. We continue, now, by repeating the last sentence that refers to the world's laws:

(1:3-6) You are not bound by them. Yet to understand that this is so, you must first realize salvation lies not there. While you would seek for it in things that have no meaning, you bind yourself to laws that make no sense. Thus do you seek to prove salvation is where it is not.

This, obviously, is a prominent theme in the Course: salvation is in our mind, not the world, and it cannot be found in a ritual, a God of form, a book, religious person, or sacred place. Salvation exists only in the decision-making mind, and so to seek for it in the mindless and dualistic world of bodies will inevitably lead to frustration and illusory thoughts of healing. The law of the mind, however, *which does heal*, is forgiveness; the reflection of God's law of perfect oneness. It is the law of shared interests as opposed to the ego's separate interests, and this undoes the ego's thought system of separation and specialness.

(3:1–5:1) Think of the freedom in the recognition that you are not bound by all the strange and twisted laws you have set up to save you. You really think that you would starve unless you have stacks of green paper strips and piles of metal discs. You really think a small round pellet or some fluid pushed into your veins through a sharpened needle will ward off disease and death. You really think you are alone unless another body is with you.

It is insanity that thinks these things. You call them laws, and put them under different names in a long catalogue of rituals that have no use and serve no purpose. You think you must obey the "laws" of medicine, of economics and of health. Protect the body and you will be saved.

These are not laws, but madness.

These laws do make perfect sense to the extent to which we identify with the body. After all, our experience tells us that bodies get sick and then get well. They get lonely and feel better when they are with other bodies, at least sometimes. And certainly if bodies do not eat, they will starve and die. Yet Jesus is not saying we should deny what our bodies need or feel, that we should not eat, take medicine if we are ill, or be with someone if we are lonely. He simply wants us to step back with him and see, within the greater context in which these laws occur (the ego's strategy of keeping us mindless), the humor in trying to protect and preserve what does not exist. Such vision being the Course's fundamental purpose is why all three of its books—text, workbook, and manual—are replete with passages like the following representative one from the text:

> [The body] suffers not the punishment you give because it has no feeling. It behaves in ways you want, but never makes the choice. It is not born and does not die. It can but follow aimlessly the path on which it has been set. And if that path is changed, it walks as easily another way (T-28.VI.2:2-6).

Zarathustra's dragon wears hundreds of thousands of scales with "Thou shalts" written on them. Yet in truth, as we have already observed, there is but one scale: *Thou shalt be an ego and shalt never look at its face again.* Out of our obedience to that ontological "thou shalt," a world arose in which we continually pay homage to this fundamental value of the ego. Where, then, *is* the ego's face? It cannot be seen in a mirror or in another, for it is only a thought in the mind. As lions, we are asked to look at the ego value of living as bodies in the world, and see how we cling to it and thus compromise reality. Jesus wants us to understand how we bend our spiritual systems to this *"Thou shalt,"* desperately trying to have God be involved in the world and thereby make the body real, not to mention prove that the body's source in the ego's wrong-minded thought system of separation is real as well. Tempting as this practice may be, it will never bring us the peace of God, for it pays homage only to the ego's deity, and its false sense of peace is always purchased at another's expense.

Again, Jesus is not encouraging us to deny our bodies or what we experience. He makes that very clear early in the text (T-2.IV.3:8-13). He wants us only to view our experience within a larger perspective, to ascend with Zarathustra above the clouds and the world's battleground and look down. When we look with him, everything is different because we do not look through the body's eyes and interpret what we see with the body's brain—all directed by the ego to make the separation real, which is the world's value of specialness. Looking through the eyes of our right minds (Christ's vision), however, everything is changed from what we had previously thought. We now perceive everything as the same, without the ego's hierarchy of illusions (T-23.II.2:3); every split mind is like every other, and we recognize that perceptual differences are insignificant, irrelevant, and a distraction from the purpose of salvation.

Much later in the workbook, Jesus discusses why we are under no laws but God's, the fundamental reason being that we are not bodies. We therefore turn to Lesson 199, "I am not a body. I am free."

"I am not a body. I am free."

In the opening paragraphs of Lesson 199, Jesus asks us to question the value we have given to our corporeal frame, which is the task of the lion. We return to the decision-making part of the mind, the location of the "I will." This frees us from being bound by the dragon's scales that represent the laws of the world. The decision-making part of the mind begins to question what the ego has told us; that having separate interests, pushing someone down in the dirt so we can be elevated, manipulating others to satisfy our emotional or physical needs, will make us feel better. In other words, the lion questions the value of *one or the other*, and assumes the right to change to new values. He is not yet ready to create or choose these, but he is at least ready to question what he had heretofore valued.

(1:1) Freedom must be impossible as long as you perceive a body as yourself.

So much for all the world's talk about freedom, which of course is not freedom anyway. Returning to what we discussed earlier, when people extol the virtues of freedom and democracy they are lying if they do not extend these virtues to *all* people. Do not believe a thing anyone tells you that reinforces separation and differentiation. This is not to say, however, that you should not vote in an election. I am only saying that we should cast our ballots with a smile on our faces, being aware that when we go into the voting booth we are voting for a liar. It does not matter to which party the candidate belongs, because he or she is not talking about freedom for *all* people. Bear in mind, too, that we believe the lies because we want to be lied to, for they preserve the ego's thought system that we have taken as our identification. And so we believe the lies others tell us because we still identify with being children of the lie.

We should therefore believe only those who speak in universals. The language may be specific, but the *content* would embrace all people, excluding no one. This means there would be no judgments made among groups of genders or sexual orientation, of racial, political, national, or religious groups, believing one is better, holier, or healthier than another. Again, why would we believe one who espoused such differences unless we wanted to make the ego thought system real? It does not matter what head of state or political party we refer to; anything that separates cannot be the truth. Therefore, the only question to ourselves should be why we still value what is not true and what openly attacks the truth.

What is so intriguing about students of *A Course in Miracles*, to focus on just one group, is that they will read again and again the Course's wonderful words about shared interests and joining, and then often proceed to erect a wall around what they read. They set it aside and then go about living their lives as if what they read meant nothing to them. This is one way of understanding the workings of the split mind. If our value does not embrace *all* people, it is inherently valueless. That is an easy rule to apply, but watch the resistance rise when we attempt to apply its principle of non-judgment. Nietzsche spoke of the terror in recognizing that we are one and that the values of the world are wrong. This is terrifying because we are still identified with the body and the self that is identified with the world's values of guilt and specialness, and do not want to let them go.

What we are questioning, once again, is not only a specific value or thing in the world, but the very self that is doing the questioning. This is the ultimate source of fear. It is very helpful to understand why the world is so resistant to this questioning in general, and why we are so resistant to it as individuals. The temptation that comes with this realization is to feel like fools for believing everything we have believed in. But we need to avoid that judgment. After all, simply coming here makes us fools. Recall the book and subsequent movie of many years ago, *Ship of Fools*. We are all on that ship because we think there *is* a ship and an ocean, and that real things occur there. Yet it is all illusion, what the great Gnostic teacher Valentinus called a *phantasmagoria*. Sure, what we do here is foolish, insane, and cruel. Still, the world remains an illusion that we share—the thought that we could be happy outside love. We know we believe this because we think we are here. This is why the undoing takes time, which is considerably shortened when we meet such evident insanity in ourselves and others with kindness and forgiveness.

Judgment is a great part of who we are. It is an inherent part of the ego thought system of separation, wherein we believe we are separate from God because we judged that we would be better off without Him. We therefore judge against love because, by its nature of total inclusion and oneness, it would undo our judgmental, special self. The ego tells us that we need to break away from the threat of Heaven's Oneness, leading us to judge against our Source, which in turn leads us to judge against ourselves for having done so. This guilt then becomes projected, and we end up judging everyone and everything, magically hoping to be free of the pain of the judgment that we are miserable sinners.

It is because judgment is an inherent part of the ego's thought system that giving it up is such a prominent theme in *A Course in Miracles*. Moreover, to give up judgment also means not to judge oneself for judging. Remember, we are being taught to *deny the denial of truth*. Judgment is the denial of truth; we deny *that* denial of truth by saying we do not want to judge anymore. This is really important. To requote these important lines:

> Call it not sin but madness.... Invest it not with guilt.... And above all, *be not afraid of it* (T-18.I.6:7-9).

We should not be calling ourselves (or others) dirty ego names simply because we are here and are foolishly indulging our specialness needs. We need only realize that specialness is a value to which we adhere and that we are always struggling to attain. Now that we are in the desert and see it as a desert, we can say and mean that we no longer want it. Thus Jesus says of the peace of God:

> To say these words [I want the peace of God]
> is nothing. But to mean these words is every-
> thing (W-pI.185.1:1-2).

This is the point. The truth is that we do not want the peace of God because of its all-inclusive nature, a reflection of Heaven's Oneness. We want the peace of the ego, which means we choose to see the Sonship in pieces, pardon the pun.

When we totally forgive ourselves, we will never judge again. The dragon is no longer dead; it will simply "cease to seem to be" (M-14.2:12). When we do not judge ourselves, which means we do not make the self-accusation of abandoning or betraying love, there will be no guilt and so nothing to project. This means we cannot judge anyone else. This frees us to look with true compassion on *all* people, because we will have realized that everyone shares the same insanity and the same terror.

(1:2) The body is a limit.

This tells us that the body is a lie, for it is a limit and was made to be a limit (T-18.VIII.1:1-4), expressing the thought of limitation—there is a place where God ends and we begin—that denies the limitless truth of Heaven. The ego's untruth limits *us*, for we are now part of a limited self that is no longer part of the All, the Oneness of Heaven. Therefore, why should we believe anything a body says when it must always express the lie of limitation?

(1:3) Who would seek for freedom in a body looks for it where it can not be found.

Freedom will never be found in the body. It will never be found in a world of bodies. It will be found only where the body is not, in the mind where God's Son is one—in illusion and in truth. When we look out from the right mind to the world, we see that everyone is the same. Beyond the disparate forms, the good *and* bad people are the same; people who suffer and those who inflict the suffering are the same. We know that everyone is the same because everyone believes he or she is a body. This is the height of insanity because it emanates from the one insane thought that we have separated from our Source.

(1:4-5) The mind can be made free when it no longer sees itself as in a body, firmly tied to it and sheltered by its presence. If this were the truth, the mind were vulnerable indeed!

If *ideas leave not their source*, and if the body is vulnerable, then the mind has to be vulnerable, too. When we realize that our minds are *in*vulnerable because of the love within them, our bodies must also be invulnerable. On the level of form, the body might be hurt, but *we are no longer the body*. Therefore it is invulnerable—not because the body itself cannot be hurt, but because *we* are not in the body. The body's vulnerability, consequently, must be illusory, since the body does not feel anything, as we have already seen.

The problem, however, is that when we consider these profound ideas it is difficult, given our bodily identification, to respond with: "What does this have to do with me?" Obviously we think we are bodies: we are reading this book with eyes, holding it with hands, writing with fingers, our brains interpreting what we are reading and cogitating its words. What helps us break this ego identification and shift to identifying with the mind is practicing the value of shared interests. To say this one more time, we do not deny we are bodies; we merely deny that our bodies are better or worse than anyone else's. This accentuates our learning we are minds, fettered only by this mind's mistaken decision.

We can view all this as an ideal toward which we grow: the top of the ladder. We see ourselves now on the lower rungs, but being led by our new teacher to ascend the ladder, gentle step by gentle step. We make our way by not seeing someone's interests as separate from our own. This holds whether we are a head of state, company, or family, or just an average person. In our minds we see only the shared purpose of learning to ascend the ladder and become a child, although we may have to behave as if our interests were indeed separate. It is almost impossible to run a business properly if we do not, but yet we can stand with Zarathustra above the clouds and laugh. We make the normal decisions a business person, parent, or citizen has to make, but we do not need to take them seriously in the sense of their affecting our peace. What we do take seriously is the value of shared interests—"together, or not at all" (T-19.IV-D.12:8)—that is beyond the dragon's scales. This is the path of the miracle that promotes our healing, leading us from the body to the mind.

As we begin to practice more and more, we will be able to de-invest from the values we gave our body and the bodies of others. Such de-investment means investing in the value in the mind, even if we are not aware of it. However, it will become increasingly clear that we are going through our daily lives as normal people do, but without being affected as we once were. We could be happy and peaceful from morning to night, regardless of external events. This does not mean that things will not happen on the bodily level and that we will not respond appropriately. It does mean, however, that the peace within our minds will stay constant. A wonderful poem of Helen's, "Awake in Stillness," begins: "Peace cover you, within without the same…" (*The Gifts of God*, p. 73). Thus we are at peace regardless of the world, and as this peace embraces us and envelops our minds, we look out through Christ's vision and our perceptions are filled with that peace, which now embraces all living things.

As I have stated many times already, we do not deny our bodies. Rather, we need to read lessons such as this and say to ourselves: "I understand the concept, but obviously I am not there yet. Still, I do want to take the steps that will lead me to my goal. I am not ready to be a child (the innocent Christ of Nietzsche's child), but I can at least continue to question the values to which I have adhered: the world's values and those of my ego's thought system of guilt and specialness." There is no reason we cannot say and mean these words, *other than that we do not want to*. The truth, then, is acknowledging our resistance to this shift. Such fear is not a sin and does not make us spiritual failures. To the contrary, it makes us honest, perhaps for the first time in our lives, for we are able to deny that we are children of the lie and affirm that the potential is there for us to reflect the truth.

(2:1) The mind that serves the Holy Spirit is unlimited forever, in all ways, beyond the laws of time and space, unbound by any preconceptions, and with strength and power to do whatever it is asked.

This right-minded choice to serve the Holy Spirit expresses Nietzsche's *will to power*. We are truly unlimited "in all ways, beyond the laws of time and space, unbound by any preconceptions, and with strength and power to do whatever it [the mind] is asked." This is the power of the *Übermensch*, the *overman*. We continue to relate to people and circumstances here, but now our peace is unaffected by them. And so we have compassion for all sentient beings—not just for the "good," but for the "bad," too; those who attack us as well as those who tell us how wonderful we are. We recognize that we are all the same. Therefore, we do not need people to praise us, because the love in our minds informs us of our inherent worth as God's Son. Similarly, it does not matter if people accuse us, because love speaks to us of our true worthiness. This is real power, and who in their right minds would not want it? Who would not want to be able to walk this world—morning to night, birth to death—with this peace?

The perverse insanity that we share is that we do *not* want this experience, preferring instead to be miserable egos, desperately trying to salvage a few crumbs from the table of specialness. This is why near the end of the text, Jesus says to us:

> Deny me not the little gift I ask [to bring our
> egos to him], when in exchange I lay before your

feet the peace of God, and power to bring this
peace to everyone who wanders in the world
uncertain, lonely, and in constant fear
(T-31.VIII.7:1).

Only the insane would turn away from such a gift. This
underscores our insanity, which leads Jesus to repeat-
edly shine his gentle light of truth on our madness.

The challenge in being a camel, in learning how to
live and do well in the world, is that we can become so
good at it that we do not want to let it go. This is always a temptation. We do not realize that being a
camel is meant only for the first part of our lives, not
its totality. Learning how to live here and embrace the
world's values, which allows us to survive, is only a
means to bring us to the end of that stage when we look
at it all and realize it is a desert that we no longer
choose to live in. Yet this is often difficult, for our resistance to the goal to which our teacher leads us is so
great. Thus even if we are in misery here, we can be
very successful at being miserable, for this enables us
to blame others, which the ego gladly encourages.

Back to the mind that is now free:

**(2:2-4) Attack thoughts cannot enter such a mind,
because it has been given to the Source of love, and
fear can never enter in a mind that has attached
itself to love. It rests in God. And who can be
afraid who lives in Innocence, and only loves?**

107

When our minds are at one with the Holy Spirit or Jesus, we accept Their value instead of the ego's. It then does not matter what people do, meaning that their attack thoughts will have no effect on our peace and we will have no attack thoughts in return. To say this another way, when our minds are filled with light, there can be no darkness, which is not an ontological state but simply the absence of the ontological state of light. Darkness is nothing in itself for it has no substance. Therefore, in the mind of the child there can be no shadows of guilt or fear.

Love in this world means being kind to all beings —animate or inanimate—because we are the same: fragments of God's one Son. Thus Jesus tells us in this rare prayer from the text:

> How holy is the smallest grain of sand, when it is recognized as being part of the completed picture of God's Son! The forms the broken pieces seem to take mean nothing. For the whole is in each one. And every aspect of the Son of God is just the same as every other part (T-28.IV.9:4-7).

Everyone deserves love because we all are a part of love, and share the same insane need to perpetuate the dream, and the same interest and goal in awakening from it. With the latter as our value there can be no specialness, and so we do not have to make ourselves holy or spiritual; in fact, we need do nothing. It is not necessary to work at forgiveness; we simply question the values we have adopted and eventually let them go, allowing the inherent value of innocence to shine forth in everyone, unimpeded by thoughts of attack. This process of forgiveness reflects Heaven's "value" of perfect Oneness.

(3) It is essential for your progress in this course that you accept today's idea ["I am not a body. I am free."], and hold it very dear. Be not concerned that to the ego it is quite insane. The ego holds the body dear because it dwells in it, and lives united with the home that it has made. It is a part of the illusion that has sheltered it from being found illusory itself.

We have all become identified with this thought system of separation and with the body that is the projection of that thought system, and so it seems insane to be told that the body is *not* who we are. Just as when Zarathustra was above the clouds, telling people it was not a thundercloud and was really nothing, deserving only laughter and dance, he was judged as mad. What is therefore so difficult is that we have made ourselves not only children of the lie, but children of madness as well. Again, this is why the process of correction takes time. A part of us screams: "No way! I am not going to the mind. I am happy to be who and where I am, even if I am miserable."

What immediately follows from our pledge to the ego is that we bring *A Course in Miracles* and Jesus to where we are. This is when the world becomes very real to us, and we feel justified in asking our inner teacher to solve problems and answer questions for us, to gently comfort us with assurances that everything is all right. At this point of course, we make Jesus different from us, which is the lie. He is *not* different from us. When we bring ourselves to him, rather than the other way around, we will let him teach us that we are inherently the same. On the other hand, when we bring him to us to solve our problems and meet our needs, we are making him different by giving him a power over us that he does not have. He cannot change our minds for us; that he can is the lie, and he does not want us to believe it. Therefore, we should not place our trust in a Jesus who fixes us, because that Jesus (a magical projection of the wish to be powerless) will root us still further in the dream, ensuring that we will never escape from it. It is this Jesus that Nietzsche railed against, and why he ridiculed the priests who claimed to represent him. Nietzsche did not know who the real Jesus was—a symbol of our right minds—but he certainly knew that the Jesus portrayed in the Bible was not anyone he wished to follow. And he was, of course, absolutely right.

The biblical Jesus, who is clearly a body, is not like us, and we should never believe those who say they are different, and that the difference makes a difference. That is the lie. We should not believe ourselves if we have a value that we think differentiates us from others. We clearly differ on the form level, but the content is always the same. God's Son is one. Therefore, the Jesus of the gospels is as much a child of the lie as everyone else because he is different. Do not confuse him with the Jesus of this course, who tells us at the beginning that he is no different from us except in time, and time does not exist (T-1.II.3:10–4:2). In the illusion of time, he is of course different, being ego free. But the only value in having him as our elder brother is that he would help us grow to become like him. And so, Jesus is the name we give to a person who appeared here, and whose body we saw and named. That name is a specific reflection of a non-specific love- and light-filled presence. This is the "spirit" in Helen's aforementioned poem "A Jesus Prayer" ("a Child, a Man, and then a Spirit"). Spirits do not have names or personalities. A child does, a man does, but a spirit does not.

Returning to the above paragraph, what is described is the ego's double shield of oblivion that is talked about in the workbook (W-pI.136.5). The ego thought system (the first shield) protects our decision-making mind from choosing love. The body (the second shield) protects the first shield by keeping us mindless. We thus get further and further away from the only power in the universe that can help us: our power to choose. All defenses are lies because they are made to protect us from fear, which itself is a lie. Since the world, then, is a defense, we should not believe any of its laws, values, or anyone who espouses them. Similarly, we should not pay attention to those who speak of spirituality in quantitative terms, which emphasizes the ego's laws of differentiation. I like to remind people that Jesus cannot count past one. There is only one valid number and one valid value—in truth and illusion.

This is why this is a very simple course. There is one ego and one Holy Spirit, shared equally by everyone. There is but one decision maker that chooses one or the other. Moreover, both alternatives are illusory since there is only one God. What could be simpler? Our goal should be to have our lives reflect that simplicity, which is accomplished by not making people different. If people were not different there could be no attack, and so the way to find real peace in this world is by not seeing people or their needs as different, by not seeing one nation-state's interests as apart from another's. This is why we should never believe the pronouncements of heads of state, for they are interested only in their nation, their government, their political ambition. All value here is derived from the law of differences, the fundamental ego lie. To be a lion, therefore, is to question and reject the world's values that are always based on separation and separate interests.

To summarize, the lion looks at the values of the world and says: "I do not want this anymore," and in so doing breaks new ground and opens the door that will allow the third stage, that of the child, to begin. To refer again to Helen's poem "A Jesus Prayer," her *child* represents Nietzsche's *camel*, the one who matures into *manhood*, becoming a *lion* who stands on its own two feet, able to step back and look at the world differently. The lions in us are ready to break new ground, letting go of the old; we do not know what will come, but we do know that we no longer desire what has come before.

An analogy to what we have been discussing can be found in the second of the three periods in Beethoven's music, of which I spoke earlier. He mastered his craft—we might say he was a wonderful camel—and this early music essentially follows the laws of the classical period. In his early thirties he discovered he was going deaf, and this launched a profound spiritual crisis. The great composer wanted to die, finding intolerable, for example, the pain of walking in his beloved Vienna woods and no longer being able to hear the birds sing, a love of nature he later immortalized in the *Pastoral* Symphony. He realized that the world and everything he had achieved to that point meant nothing. Yet he drew upon his inner strength as a lion, and what emerged was the *Eroica* Symphony, a "lionesque" symphony if there ever were one. It begins with two strong E-flat chords that, in effect, shattered music as the world had known it. This third symphony initiated Beethoven's middle period, from which emanated his most famous music: the Fifth and Sixth Symphonies, the opera *Fidelio*, and many sonatas and quartets among other compositions. In that period, then, he broke new ground.

There is a story, perhaps apocryphal, that says that as Beethoven lay dying, there was a clap of thunder. The musical titan rose up from the bed, clenched his fist and shook it at the heavens, as if to say: "You are not going to get me!" That is the lion, the fighter, the one that says the world will no longer be the same because he does not believe in it anymore. Out of this come new forms: "Down with the old, and up with the new!" This mighty transition, however, is often accompanied by anxiety, a resistance to the truth we know lies within us, a part of us fearfully exclaiming, as did Beethoven in his early desire for death: "I am not going any further!"

What makes the spiritual path so difficult, therefore, is our fear of a future that means letting go of our self, the value we place on our special existence. This fear compels us to protect that specialness, which we do by attacking others. This inevitably gives rise to the principle of *one or the other*, the belief in separate interests that gave birth to the ego and sustains it. How could our interests be shared if our life is predicated on putting another down? How could we have a common goal if our very life is contingent upon breathing air that destroys thousands of microorganisms, or eating something that once lived? How can existence be one if our emotional needs are satisfied only by using others so that we have what once belonged to them? It is this fear that cries out: *Who would I be without my ego? What would I be without my specialness?* We are not talking about dying physically by not eating or breathing, but about letting go of a thought system. Yet despite this fear it is possible for us at least to begin the process of questioning the value of these ego principles.

As we close this chapter, it is important to keep in mind that Nietzsche's stages are presented as three discrete stages, as are the six stages in the development of trust (M-4.I). Despite this, they really represent a more ambiguous and fluid process in which we gradually "loose the world from all [we] thought it was" (W-pI.132). Nonetheless, we can say that within any one stage we go back and forth—from the right to the wrong mind, and vice versa. In this process of vacillation, we let go of the world's values, and then become afraid and embrace them again. This calls to mind the passage near the end of "The Obstacles to Peace" that depicts our standing before the final veil, ready to pass through to God. Then fear takes over and our eyes look down, remembering the promise to our "friends"—sin, guilt, fear, and death (T-19.IV-D.6). As we make our way up the ladder and advance on the journey, we become increasingly aware of our right-minded changes, so that now when we become fright-ened and return to our ego state, we know it and thus do not stay there as long. We say, then, that we do not want to live in the ego's world anymore; it hurts too much. When we have an increasing taste of the experi-ence of love and peace, why would we ever want to change it for guilt and conflict?

Finally, since the spatial world of linear time itself is illusory, spiritual progress as a temporal concept is an illusion too. We identify with bodies, and bodies live in a world of time and space. Thus, even though the process we are discussing occurs in the mind, be-yond the world, we must still deal with our experi-ence within the framework of the temporal-spatial dimension. We therefore need to talk about the pro-cess as though it were sequential, at the same time re-membering that it is not that way at all.

5. Stage Three: The Child

We move now to Nietzsche's third stage, that of the child. To review: The first stage is our growing up in the world, followed by the second stage that is marked by our beginning to question the values of the world and ending in our "slaying" of the dragon. The camel thus becomes a lion who is able to create freedom for himself, but is not able to create new values. He has won the freedom to choose, which is what Nietzsche meant by the *will to power*, the mind's ability to choose between the valuable and the valueless, the Holy Spirit and the ego, Heaven and hell. Once the old has been undone and the dragon (the ego) disposed of, the third stage has been reached. One has chosen against the wrong mind, which leaves only the right mind, the pure world of the child.

Here is what Nietzsche says of this transition. Note how he gives very little attention to the child; it is really just one short paragraph.

The Lion Becomes the Child

But say, my brothers, what can the child do that even the lion could not do? Why must the preying lion still become a child?

In other words, why does this great beast that has done away with the dragon and its scales of "thou shalts" still need another metamorphosis?

The child is innocence and forgetting, a new beginning, a game, a self-propelled wheel, a first movement, a sacred "Yes." For the game of creation, my brothers, a sacred "Yes" is needed: the spirit now wills his own will, and he who had been lost to the world now conquers his own world.

From the perspective of *A Course in Miracles* we would say that the child forgets what never was. Nietzsche is speaking of the preparation for attaining the real world, the state of mind when one has irrevocably chosen *against* the ego and *for* the Holy Spirit.

One does not do anything to have this stage emerge. The work actually occurs between the stage of the lion and the child, which is not really discussed here. We see that clearly expressed, however, in the "Development of Trust" section in the manual, specifically in Jesus' discussion of the fifth stage.* Remember, there is no counterpart to the camel in those six stages. The lion essentially refers to stages one through four, the first three involving the recognition that what had heretofore seemed valuable is

---

* See the Appendix, p. 155.

now deemed valueless. Once that choice is clear, what remains is peace, the fourth stage when the lion is able to say, "I will," and recognizes that he now has the power to choose. He is the dreamer of the dream instead of the dream figure. Yet if we pay careful attention, as discussed earlier, we notice it is *I* will, meaning there is still a sense of self. Even though we are talking about a spiritual power, there remains a sense of a self doing something. It is thus not a state of pure being, but still a state of choosing. This is why the fourth stage is not the end of the journey, and why in describing it, Jesus says:

> The teacher of God needs this period of respite. He has not yet come as far as he thinks (M-4.I.6:9-10).

One could think of this fourth stage as the part of the process when one learns that "Forgiveness is the key to happiness" (W-pI.121), that we are far better off practicing forgiveness than judgment. We begin to see the real value of shared instead of separate interests, and realize that on the level of the mind we are the same. Yet there is still a sense of self and personal identity. The lion, after all, is not a self that can be ignored. There is a tremendous sense of power for it is no longer bound by the world. Nonetheless, this is not the journey's end for though we are living in a happy dream of forgiveness, to be preferred to the ego's nightmare dreams of guilt and attack, we still sleep. This stage is therefore an experience of a peace that is untouched, despite what goes on around us, but there remains a sense of *I*.

The sixth stage, which is comparable to Nietzsche's child, is the attainment of the real world, but one does not move from the fourth to the sixth stage without undergoing the fifth, and that is when all hell breaks loose, so to speak. As Jesus describes it, we have not *fully* understood the difference between the valuable and the valueless, because we have not looked at the inherent valuelessness of our very self. The end of the journey, therefore, is not the right-minded self that lives more happily, peacefully, and kindly within the dream. While certainly a better place to be than the first three stages, and far better than being in the desert, it still does not awaken us from the dream and lead us home. The ultimate goal of this course is to end the dream, not to have us live better within it. Recall that Jesus gives us a counterpart to this stage in describing how the Holy Spirit leads us through the circle of fear, with God being beyond it (T-18.IX.3:7-9). The circle of fear represents this fifth stage, the realization that our fundamental value is having a separated self; not just being less judgmental, anxious, or depressed, but valuing the self itself.

This is the same kind of thinking that we find near the end of the text when Jesus tells us that the problem is not *what* we think, but *that* we think (T-31.V.14); the problem is not really whether we are right- or wrong-minded, but that we think there is a self that can be right- or wrong-minded. *A Course in Miracles* will lead us to the gate of Heaven, just before which is the real world. Beyond that gate is God, the end of the journey that never was. In the real world there is no longer a sense of self because we are outside the dream, no longer a figure within the dream. Jesus describes this in several places in the text, and in one passage explains that we are in the real world but an instant, with just barely enough time to thank God for it, and then the dream is over as God reaches down and lifts us back unto Himself (T-17.II.4:4-5). This, of course, is only a metaphor to describe a process that cannot be described except through symbols.

Thus *the real world* is the Course's term for the state of the illusory mind when it recognizes that everything of the ego is an illusion. The wrong mind is an illusion, and so it disappears. The right mind, which is the correction for the illusion, is no longer needed because it has already corrected the wrong mind, and so that disappears too. Finally, the decision-making part of the mind is now unnecessary and irrelevant because there is nothing to choose between. No

121

wrong mind, no right mind, no decision maker—the whole self is gone. This is when we enter into the real world. We have chosen once and for all to deny the ego's reality and to affirm that only the Holy Spirit's Atonement is true. In the other five stages we vacillate, but this sixth and final stage is permanent. This is the child of Nietzsche's parable and the spirit in Helen's poem "A Jesus Prayer."

The child is innocence, which means there is no sin and no guilt—nothing happened to change the Unchangeable: "... not one note in Heaven's song was missed" (T-26.V.5:4). Nothing altered reality; there was no separation, no break in the Godhead. Love flows as it always has, for nothing has interfered with the innocence of Christ. This truth, called the Atonement in *A Course in Miracles*, undoes the ego's tale that God's Son is guilty. Accepting the Atonement means forgetting everything the ego has taught. Indeed, the Holy Spirit teaches us to forget what we remembered, which is the ego's thought system, and to remember what we forgot, which is Who we are as Christ (e.g., T-5.II.6:1; T-12.II.2). Again, "The child is innocence and forgetting, a new beginning, a game...." The use of the word *game* goes hand in hand with Zarathustra dancing, laughing, singing—not taking the world seriously. Thus we look at the *tiny, mad idea* and remember to laugh instead of forgetting to do so.

The split mind, therefore, can be thought of as including both the ego's and Holy Spirit's way of looking at the *tiny, mad idea*. The ego is thrilled by it, and revels in the freedom it believes it has won. When the decision maker turns to the Holy Spirit, however, it joins in the soft smile that gently dismisses the ego and its insane thought system of separation. This smile conveys the thought that nothing happened and we are still at home in God. This is the essence of Nietzsche's message, the correction for the seriousness the world seems to hold and the seriousness with which we look at the world. It is a new beginning, a first movement. "It is a self-propelled wheel," meaning that it is *my* power, *my* will that propels the wheel; the *my* being the decision-making self that has finally made the choice for Self over self. In Nietzsche's system, despite the fact of living in a world of *eternal recurrence* where the same things happen over and over, the *Übermensch* (the overman) is above them all and unaffected by their seeming power. Combining Nietzsche and *A Course in Miracles*, we can say that the *Übermensch* does not change the world—how can what does not exist change?—and is not affected by it either, being above the vicissitudes of life. This advanced teacher of God simply looks down upon the unreal and dances, laughing at what appear to be tragically serious thunderclouds, thereby ushering in the real world.

Those in the real world, as Jesus was, know they are not here. People may see and relate to the body that appears, but in the real world we know we are outside the dream. When Christians recounted the phenomenon of Jesus, they got it totally wrong because they talked of someone who was here in a body. Moreover, not only was he physically here, but he was part of his Father's grand plan of atonement. This is why we should not believe what we read in the Bible; it is based on a lie. When Jesus appeared in the world he knew he was not here. His message to us was to come to where he was, to be the eternal child. Yet instead of joining Jesus outside the dream, the world brought him into the dream, thus preserving its seeming reality and saying no to the truth.

The "Sacred Yes"

Up to now we have been camels and lions. The camel says yes to the world, not realizing that this yes is really a negation, a no to the truth. The world is this yes, and we all affirm this negation of the truth. The lion, then, is when we suddenly recognize that the camel—the ego—has brought us into a desert that we no longer wish to remain in. We therefore say no to the world's yes to negating the truth. The lion thus cancels out this negation; it *denies the denial of truth* (T-12.II.1:5). We say "not no," and this means yes to the truth (T-21.VII.12:4). When the ego's negation is undone, what is left is the "sacred yes." The Course's understanding of Nietzsche's "sacred yes" is the affirmation of life itself, but not the world's life. The ultimate "sacred yes" is to the reality of God and His Love.

We do not make this yes happen. It happens of itself to the extent that we realize that the lion is not the final step. Repeating an earlier point, the problem is that it feels so good to be a lion; we quickly forget our spiritual goal and that the lion is only a stage on a journey. Losing sight of that, the *will to power* (or the will to choose) gets quickly transmuted into a will to dominate—a power that overpowers and destroys. The temptation is great, as the religious history of the world attests, for this power often entraps our spiritual leaders. We get an inkling of that *will to power*—the power of the mind to choose—and then quickly identify with it: It is *my* will. This is the meaning behind the famous statement of Lord Acton: "All power corrupts and absolute power corrupts absolutely." We still lack humility, and do not realize that humility was an important component of the first stage. It is also important in the second because it brings us to the third.

As an example of this, very soon after *A Course in Miracles* was published, people began to use it as a weapon against others. I remember sometime in the mid-seventies when the Course was just barely out, Helen, Bill, Judy Skutch, and I traveled to a southern state and met a man who obviously had been traumatized by experiences with his Church as he was growing up. He had made a chart outlining point by point how the Course refuted everything that the Bible and his Church taught. He was all set to race to his minister and confront him with what Jesus *really* said. Helen stopped him, fortunately, although I do not know what happened later on. This is an example of the misuse of power. We feel good because we realize that the values of the world do not work. Yet, if we believe that it is incumbent upon us to present this truth to others by humiliating, embarrassing, or proving them wrong, Zarathustra's words are apposite: even when we know we are right, we would be wrong. When we feel compelled to do something, when there is a strong sense of *I*, when we think we have the truth, we need to recall that we do not.

The ego's thought system of specialness is all about *differences*: You are different from me; you have been misguided and I am not; I have the truth and it is in this holy book. This is when we know we are mistaken, for we claim that the other person is wrong. The truth is that we are the same, as we are reminded in this New Year's Prayer from the Course:

> Make this year different by making it all the same (T-15.XI.10:11).

In confronting others, we are using a course that teaches the inherent sameness of God's Son as a weapon to prove how different we are, and how different the Course is from what other people are teaching and believing. This is not about objective comparison. To be sure, *A Course in Miracles* teaches a different form of the universal message from the Bible, but we do not have to judge or condemn those who follow the Bible. We do not have to go out of our way to prove other people wrong, especially since the underlying motivation for doing so is to make ourselves right at their expense.

That is why, as we recall, Jesus asks us:

> Do you prefer that you be right or happy? (T-29.VII.1:9)

When we want to be right, we will never be happy, because needing to be right means we have proven that someone else is mistaken. This in turn means we have proven that differences are real. How could we be happy then, for we would have identified with an insane thought system. Moreover, when we have to prove that other people are wrong and we are right, and we use the "holy word" to do so, we are reinforcing our guilt. We will have accused ourselves once again of betraying the Oneness of God's Love by affirming the truth of individuality and separation. The way to prove that what we believe is true is by our love. I frequently quote this wonderful line from the text:

> Teach not that I died in vain. Teach rather that I
> did not die by demonstrating that I live in you
> (T-11.VI.7:3-4).

We do not teach Jesus' words or his theory; we *demonstrate* their truth by letting his love teach through us. This is Nietzsche's child of innocence, which reflects Heaven's Oneness. If there is separation there are differences, which means there is sin; sin being the insane belief in the reality of the separation. And if sin is real, so too must guilt be. How can there be innocence then, which is equated with oneness? And so whenever we catch ourselves trying to prove someone else is mistaken, and we have an investment in doing so, we should stop and ask our Teacher for help. The power of the lion lies in its gentleness, not in its ability to dominate, and this characteristic (the fourth in the manual's description of an advanced teacher of God [M-4.IV]) marks the transition to the child.

Implicit in the process of becoming a child is that there is no longer an *I*, since we are outside the dream of individuality and specialness. This, incidentally, is why in the real world there is no one named Jesus; as we saw, the non-specific has no name (see p. 111). However, this is not something we need to focus on. The shift to the real world will automatically happen to the extent that we are able to get our personal selves out of the way. And all we need do to make this happen is to be aware of our need to see differences and make people wrong. Thus our focus is on being able to see that everyone shares the same insane thought system, as well as the need to awaken from that thought system. We do not seek to change the ego; we simply become aware of our temptation to do so. It is helpful to notice how comfortable we are in criticizing others and becoming angry or depressed. This may seem counterintuitive, but the fact is that we unconsciously choose such thoughts in order to be the victim, and so value our feelings of anger or misery. Being aware of the causal connection between our decision to be sick, attacking, or anxious, and the unhappy effects that inevitably follow that decision, is sufficient to shift our identity from the ego's judgments to the Holy Spirit's forgiveness.

There is a part of us that understands all this, and yet we do not like it. It comes down to a question of what we value. This is where Nietzsche's system is helpful because it directs our focus toward our values. We value ourselves, even though we are aware on some level that this perverse self-esteem prevents us from returning to our non-dualistic home where our self unites with Self and the separated *I* disappears. Even though part of us truly desires that, the other part is terrified, and this is what freezes us on the ladder. That fear often manifests itself physically or psychologically in our becoming sick, angry, depressed, or harboring feelings of hopelessness.

These reactions are self-protective, the ego's ways of trying to protect its existence, echoed in Lesson 136, "Sickness is a defense against the truth." Anything—illness, anger, depression, anxiety, etc.— is a defense against the truth because it paralyzes us in our journey. We are afraid that if we continue, we will vanish. It is helpful to understand that the *I* is gone only at the very end, and, again, this is not our concern. What disappears as we move along is our disquiet, unhappiness, and loneliness, leaving us with a heightened sense of well being. The journey concludes when we recognize that even this happiness is not enough, for we want to be totally free of anything that reflects duality. But no one is rushing us or pushing us to that awareness.

The Child in Us

Let us look now at parts of Lesson 182, "I will be still an instant and go home," which talk about the child. The first three paragraphs describe our experience of feeling like aliens here—that this world is not our home. Jesus says that everyone knows what he is speaking of, and then he shifts the discussion midway through paragraph 4:

(4:3) Yet there is a Child in you Who seeks His Father's house, and knows that He is alien here.

"Child" is capitalized as it refers to the Christ in us or, for the purpose of our discussion, the memory of Who we are as Christ, the desire to return to our true Self.

Knowing we are alien here is the lion recognizing that the world has no real meaning. This world is a desert, where, as we recall, "starved and thirsty creatures come to die" (W-pII.13.5:1). This is not a place we wish to make our home. This awareness opens our minds to embrace our true home, the Heaven wherein we live forever:

(4:4-6) This childhood is eternal, with an inno-cence that will endure forever. Where this Child shall go is holy ground. It is His Holiness that lights up Heaven, and that brings to earth the pure reflection of the light above, wherein are earth and Heaven joined as one.

This is the end of the journey, when what is re-flected becomes what was being reflected. In the con-text of healing, Jesus speaks of the journey's conclusion in this way:

> Those who have learned to offer only healing, because of the reflection of holiness in them, are ready at last for Heaven. There, holiness is not a reflection, but rather the actual condition of what was but reflected to them here. God is no image, and His creations, as part of Him, hold Him in them in truth. They do not merely reflect truth, for they *are* truth (T-14.IX.8:4-7).

Therefore, in order to become the love that is only re-flected here, we need to see the innocence of God's Son—the holy eternal Child Who is our Self—in everyone we meet, without exception. In this way the Oneness of Heaven joins with the sameness of all who walk the earth. And Heaven's light shines ever brighter as each seemingly fragmented Son returns to the home he never left.

(8:1) When you are still an instant, when the world recedes from you, when valueless ideas cease to have value in your restless mind, then will you hear His Voice.

In this passage, "His Voice" belongs to the Child, the same as the Holy Spirit's Voice. Yet we cannot hear It as long as valueless ideas remain important to us. Again, the role of the lion is no longer to value what is valueless (W-pI.133)—thoughts of specialness or individuality, of being right. These are valueless because they do not make us happy, and all Jesus asks of us is the little willingness to choose the holy instant and question what we have heretofore held as valuable.

(8:2-3) So poignantly He calls to you that you will not resist Him longer. In that instant He will take you to His home, and you will stay with Him in perfect stillness, silent and at peace, beyond all words, untouched by fear and doubt, sublimely certain that you are at home.

This is the consummation of the spiritual path, when it is no longer the Child leading us, for we will have *become* the Child. As Jesus says in several places in the Course, this is beyond what he is teaching us (e.g., T-18.IX.11; W-pI.161.4; W-pI.169.10). In fact, this cannot be taught (W-pI.157.9). What he does teach us, however, is not to value what is valueless; to become a lion. The focus of *A Course in Miracles*, then, is on how to look at the world and know that it is not what we want, recalling Lesson 128, "The world I see holds nothing that I want."

Importantly, Jesus is not talking about the world, but about that of which the world is a projection: the thought system of guilt that made it (T-13.in.2:2). On a practical day-in-and-day-out basis, questioning our values means realizing that we are all the same—having shared rather than separate interests—thus seeing the unity behind the ego's false perception of differences.

(12:1) You have not lost your innocence.

Our innocence has not been lost, because it is always there. We can think of the Holy Spirit as the memory of our innocence as Christ. The problem is that this innocence has been covered over by guilt, and the guilt covered over by the world of guilt. What is guilt? Separation. What is the world of guilt? Separate interests. Thus guilt and the perception of differences constitute the ego's double shield of oblivion that prevents us from gaining access to the memory of innocence that transcends all differences, and therefore transcends sin.

(12:2-3) It is for this you yearn. This is your heart's desire.

Implied in this statement is Jesus asking us: "Why would you want anything but your innocence? Why would you choose what the world of specialness offers you?" The fulfillment of our special needs and desires will never bring us the peace of God, and will not return us to the state of innocence we believe we threw away, yet for which we still yearn. Specialness, by its very nature, separates and makes people different; our needs differentiate us from others, whom we need to satisfy us. Yet we will never find happiness in separation, nor remember the innocence that is born in oneness. This innocence *is* our "heart's desire," the only true value within a valueless world.

(12:4-9) This is the voice [of the Child] you hear, and this the call which cannot be denied. The holy Child remains with you. His home is yours. Today He gives you His defenselessness, and you accept it in exchange for all the toys of battle you have made. And now the way is open, and the journey has an end in sight at last. Be still an instant and go home with Him, and be at peace a while.

What is helpful when we read a passage like this—we will see an equally beautiful passage shortly—is recognizing that the Child's innocence is what we really want, what we truly yearn for. We then see the magnitude of our insanity that we would

135

throw this away for the little crumbs of specialness that we believe have such great value, and which we defend with such silly "toys of battle." These crumbs work very well in the first part of our life—childhood, adolescence, and early adulthood—for they accomplish things in the world. We therefore should be grateful because these are the steppingstones of the curriculum that Jesus will use to take us home.

Now our eyes are open and we see specialness for the desert it is. Our anger and judgments ("the toys of battle")—however justified they seem to be—mean that we are still fighting against the world's dragons, and this desire to fight is what keeps us in the desert. Why, Jesus continually asks, would we not exchange the ego's measly offerings for the banquet of love he holds out for us as he leads us to our home and the stillness of his peace?

Identifying with the Child

The last two paragraphs in Lesson 187, "I bless the world because I bless myself," describe what happens when we identify with the Child Who is our Self.

(10:1-3) Now are we one in thought, for fear has gone. And here, before the altar to one God, one Father, one Creator and one Thought, we stand

together as one Son of God. Not separate from Him Who is our Source; not distant from one brother who is part of our one Self Whose innocence has joined us all as one, we stand in blessedness, and give as we receive.

The message here is hard to miss. Since blessed innocence is what we truly want, we need to recall that thought each and every time we are tempted to make differences real—to criticize, mock, prove another wrong, or want to change someone. How could we change a person who is one with us? We do so only when we think that person is different. And so we need continually to bring together the thought of differences and the thought of oneness (note, incidentally, the nine *ones* in the above three sentences). This will move us through these stages to our goal of being the innocent child. Yet as we know, *we* do not do it. Our part is simply to look at these two thoughts with Jesus, for this enables us to choose one and let the other go. Recall this earlier line from the text:

> The way out of conflict between two opposing thought systems is clearly to choose one and relinquish the other (T-6.V-B.5:1).

To do this we must see the conflict, for how else could we choose between two thought systems if we do not know we have them? How could we escape conflict if we do not even know we are in conflict? If we believe differences are real and the fragmented Sonship is reality, we are in conflict with the truth; a totally untenable position. We then try to defend ourselves against this truth—what we did at the beginning with God and are still doing—because we are defending the ego's separated self we know to be untrue.

(10:4) The Name of God is on our lips.

"The Name of God" is the theme of Lessons 183 and 184. Yet the Name is never given because God does not have one. God's "Name" is our Identity as part of His perfect Oneness. There are not two identities in Heaven, for there is only one Self, and so God's Name is our Identity and inheritance, as those lessons teach. His Name is the Name of Oneness: God *and* Son. If the "Name of God is on our lips," we need only watch ourselves seek to deny and shatter that oneness when we choose to be angry, judgmental, or manipulative—symptoms of the specialness that would separate and fragment the Son that God created one with Him.

(10:5) And as we look within, we see the purity of Heaven shine in our reflection of our Father's Love.

This reflection is the perfect child of innocence, the third metamorphosis. Its love and oneness, with which we now identify, gently extend through us to embrace all who believe they are children of separation and guilt.

(11:1-4) Now are we blessed, and now we bless the world. What we have looked upon we would extend, for we would see it everywhere. We would behold it shining with the grace of God in everyone. We would not have it be withheld from anything we look upon.

"We would not have it be withheld from anything we look upon." That is the key. If we read and understand no other sentence but this in *A Course in Miracles*, we will have gotten its message of forgiveness. This would allow us to forgive ourselves as we watch our attempts to withhold God's grace—the reflection of His Love—from anything and everything we look upon. When we attack one person we attack everyone, because we are destroying the perfect unity and wholeness of the Sonship. This all-inclusiveness of the mind's content—attack or forgiveness—is what makes the Course so difficult. Our very self is built upon the belief in differences and exclusivity. Bodies were made to be different and so we think we are bodies. Thus we made a world of billions upon billions of bodies, each one belonging to a particular species, with multitudinous differences within each one. Since the body is our identification, it is very hard to overcome our resistance to stepping aside from it. This is why, within the illusion of temporal reality, undoing the ego's thought system takes time.

Once we realize the innate valuelessness of everything here, and feel the innate value of the love within, the blessings of peace automatically extend through us. *We* do not bless the world, and if we think we do, the blessing becomes a curse. Instead, we seek to have the blessing flow through us by getting out of its way. Yet if we find ourselves interfering with its extension by directing it, telling Jesus who should and should not be blessed, or deriving personal gain, we know for certain that we are back in the ego's land of curses, specialness, and separate interests.

(11:5) And to ensure this holy sight is ours, we offer it to everything we see.

Jesus says this in case we missed the previous line, "We would not have it be withheld from anything we look upon." The "holy sight" is the vision of Christ, the true perception of the Holy Spirit. "And to ensure this holy sight is ours, we offer it to everything we see." This means *everything*; not some, and looks ahead to Jesus' final vision:

Yet this a vision is which you must share with
everyone you see, for otherwise you will behold
it not (T-31.VIII.8:5).

It is most instructive to see how often Jesus uses
words such as *everything*, *all*, and *every* throughout
A Course in Miracles. This all-inclusiveness is the
principal characteristic of the innocent child. Remember, innocence means there is no guilt. If there is
no guilt, there is no separation. If there is no separation, then we remain the one Son that God created
one with His Love. We then need to watch how we
try to subvert this simple truth; how we try to get
God, the Holy Spirit, or Jesus on our side to agree
with us; for example, certain people deserve a blessing and others do not. This is why in the famous gospel
crucifixion scene both the good and bad thieves are on
crosses. There is always the good and the bad, the
sheep and the goats, the saved and the damned. Once
again, we should never believe anyone or anything
that preaches differences.

**(11:6) For where we see it, it will be returned to us
in form of lilies we can lay upon our altar, making
it a home for Innocence Itself, Who dwells in us
and offers us His Holiness as ours.**

Innocence Itself is God, and lilies are the Course's
great symbol of forgiveness, which we lay upon the

altar of our minds and offer its innocence to everyone we meet or even think about, without exception. In this way we prepare our minds for God, having given welcome to the truth (W-pII.14.3:7). We have completed our part of the journey by moving beyond the ego's unholy world of separate interests to Jesus' world of reflected holiness: the innocence of the child, God's Son whose light shines in all the seeming fragments of the dream.

6. Closing: The Birth of the Child in Us

A fitting close to our discussion is Helen's lovely poem "The Hope of Christmas." Helen had written this as a Christmas gift for a good friend of ours who was a priest. The poem uses Christmas symbols to refer to the birth of the Child in all of us, the goal to which *A Course in Miracles* gently leads us. The journey that took us from and through the camel's world joyously ends in our return to the comforting Arms that have never ceased to embrace us in their love.

The Hope of Christmas

Christ is not born but neither does He die,
And yet He is reborn in everyone.
The rising and the birth are one in Him,
For it is in the advent of God's Son
The light of resurrection is begun.

Heaven needs no nativity. And yet
The Son of Heaven needs the world to be
His birthplace, for the world is overcome
Because a Child is born. And it is He
Who brings God's promise of eternity.

6. CLOSING: THE BIRTH OF THE CHILD IN US

It is His birth that ends the dream of death,
For in Him death is brought to life. Behold
the earth made new and shining in the hope
Of love and pardon. Now God's Arms enfold
The hearts that shivered in the winter's cold.

(The Gifts of God, p. 98)

APPENDIX

"On the Three Metamorphoses"
From *Thus Spoke Zarathustra*
(translated by Walter Kaufmann)
Friedrich Nietzsche

Of three metamorphoses of the spirit I tell you: how the spirit becomes a camel; and the camel, a lion; and the lion, finally, a child.

There is much that is difficult for the spirit, the strong reverent spirit that would bear much: but the difficult and the most difficult are what its strength demands.

What is difficult? asks the spirit that would bear much, and kneels down like a camel wanting to be well loaded. What is most difficult, O heroes, asks the spirit that would bear much, that I may take it upon myself and exult in my strength? Is it not humbling oneself to wound one's haughtiness? Letting one's folly shine to mock one's wisdom?

Or is it this: parting from our cause when it triumphs? Climbing high mountains to tempt the tempter?

Or is it this: feeding on the acorns and grass of knowledge and, for the sake of the truth, suffering hunger in one's soul?

Or is it this: being sick and sending home the comforters and making friends with the deaf, who never hear what you want?

Or is it this: stepping into filthy waters when they are the waters of truth, and not repulsing cold frogs and hot toads?

Or is it this: loving those who despise us and offering a hand to the ghost that would frighten us?

All these most difficult things the spirit that would bear much takes upon itself: like the camel that, burdened, speeds into the desert, thus the spirit speeds into its desert.

In the loneliest desert, however, the second metamorphosis occurs: here the spirit becomes a lion who would conquer his freedom and be master in his own desert. Here he seeks out his last master: he wants to fight him and his last god; for ultimate victory he wants to fight with the great dragon.

Who is the great dragon whom the spirit will no longer call lord and god? "Thou shalt" is the name of the great dragon. But the spirit of the lion says, "I will." "Thou shalt" lies in his way, sparkling like gold, an animal covered with scales; and on every scale shines a golden "thou shalt."

Values, thousands of years old, shine on these scales; and thus speaks the mightiest of all dragons: "All value of all things shines on me. All value has long been created, and I am all created value. Verily, there shall be no more 'I will.'" Thus speaks the dragon.

My brothers, why is there a need in the spirit for the lion? Why is not the beast of burden, which renounces and is reverent, enough?

To create new values—that even the lion cannot do; but the creation of freedom for oneself for new creation—that is within the power of the lion. The creation of freedom for oneself and a sacred "No" even to duty—for that, my brothers, the lion is needed. To assume the right to new values—that is the most terrifying assumption for a reverent spirit that would bear much. Verily, to him it is preying, and a matter for a beast of prey. He once loved "thou shalt" as most sacred: now he must find illusion and caprice even in the most sacred, that freedom from his love may become his prey; the lion is need for such prey.

But say, my brothers, what can the child do that even the lion could not do? Why must the preying lion still become a child? The child is innocence and forgetting, a new beginning, a game, a self-propelled wheel, a first movement, a sacred "Yes." For the game of creation, my brothers, a sacred "Yes" is needed: the spirit now wills his own will, and he who had been lost to the world now conquers his own world.

Of three metamorphoses of the spirit I have told you: how the spirit became a camel; and the camel, a lion; and the lion, finally a child.

Thus spoke Zarathustra.

A Jesus Prayer

A Child, a Man and then a Spirit, come
In all Your loveliness. Unless You shine
Upon my life, it is a loss to You,
And what is loss to You is also mine.

I cannot calculate why I am here
Except for this: I know that I have come
To seek You here and find You. In Your life
You show the way to my eternal home.

A child, a man and then a spirit. So
I follow in the way You show to me
That I may come at last to be like You.
What but Your likeness would I want to be?

There is a silence where You speak to me
And give me words of love to say for You
To those You send to me. And I am blessed
Because in them I see You shining through.

There is no gratitude that I can give
For such a gift. The light around Your head
Must speak for me, for I am dumb beside
Your gentle hand with which my soul is led.

I take Your gift in holy hands, for You
Have blessed them with Your own. Come,
   brothers, see
How like to Christ am I, and I to you
Whom He has blessed and holds as one with me.

A perfect picture of what I can be
You show to me, that I might help renew
Your brothers' failing sight. As they look up
Let them not look on me, but only You.

(Helen Schucman, *The Gifts of God*, pp. 82-83)

"Development of Trust"
The Six Stages of Spiritual Development in the
Advanced Teachers of God
(From the Manual for Teachers, M-4.I.3-8)

First, they [teachers of God] must go through what might be called "a period of undoing." This need not be painful, but it usually is so experienced. It seems as if things are being taken away, and it is rarely understood initially that their lack of value is merely being recognized. How can lack of value be perceived unless the perceiver is in a position where he must see things in a different light? He is not yet at a point at which he can make the shift entirely internally. And so the plan will sometimes call for changes in what seem to be external circumstances. These changes are always helpful. When the teacher of God has learned that much, he goes on to the second stage.

Next, the teacher of God must go through "a period of sorting out." This is always somewhat difficult because, having learned that the changes in his life are always helpful, he must now decide all things on the basis of whether they increase the helpfulness or hamper it. He will find that many, if not most of the things he valued before will merely hinder his ability to transfer what he has learned to new situations as they arise. Because he has valued what is really valueless, he will not generalize the lesson for fear of loss and sacrifice. It takes great learning to understand that all things, events, encounters and circumstances are helpful. It is only to the extent to which they are helpful that any degree of reality should be accorded them in this world of illusion. The word "value" can apply to nothing else.

The third stage through which the teacher of God must go can be called "a period of relinquishment." If this is interpreted as giving up the desirable, it will engender enormous conflict. Few teachers of God escape this distress entirely. There is, however, no point in sorting out the valuable from the valueless unless the next obvious step is taken. Therefore, the period of overlap is apt to be one in which the teacher of God feels called upon to sacrifice his own best interests on behalf of truth. He has not realized as yet how wholly impossible such a demand would be. He can learn this only as he actually does give up the valueless. Through this, he learns that where he anticipated grief, he finds a happy lightheartedness instead; where he thought something was asked of him, he finds a gift bestowed on him.

Now comes "a period of settling down." This is a quiet time, in which the teacher of God rests a while in reasonable peace. Now he consolidates his learning. Now he begins to see the transfer value of what he has learned. Its potential is literally staggering, and the teacher of God is now at the point in his progress at which he sees in it his whole way out. "Give up what you do not want, and keep what you do." How simple is the obvious! And how easy to do! The teacher of God needs this period of respite. He has not yet come as far as he thinks. Yet when he is ready to go on, he goes with mighty companions beside him. Now he rests a while, and gathers them before going on. He will not go on from here alone.

The next stage is indeed "a period of unsettling." Now must the teacher of God understand that he did not really know what was valuable and what was valueless. All that he really learned so far was that he did not want the valueless, and that he did want the valuable. Yet his own sorting out was meaningless in teaching him the difference. The idea of sacrifice, so central to his own thought system, had made it impossible for him to judge. He thought he learned willingness, but now he sees that he does not know what the willingness is for. And now he must attain a state that may remain impossible to reach for a long, long time. He must learn to lay all judgment aside, and ask only what he really wants in every circumstance. Were not each step in this direction so heavily reinforced, it would be hard indeed!

155

And finally, there is "a period of achievement." It is here that learning is consolidated. Now what was seen as merely shadows before become solid gains, to be counted on in all "emergencies" as well as tranquil times. Indeed, the tranquility is their result; the outcome of honest learning, consistency of thought and full transfer. This is the stage of real peace, for here is Heaven's state fully reflected. From here, the way to Heaven is open and easy. In fact, it is here. Who would "go" anywhere, if peace of mind is already complete? And who would seek to change tranquility for something more desirable? What could be more desirable than this?

INDEX OF REFERENCES TO *A COURSE IN MIRACLES*

text

text (continued)

text (continued)

workbook for students

The Gifts of God

Foundation for *A Course in Miracles*®

Kenneth Wapnick *received his Ph.D. in Clinical Psychology in 1968 from Adelphi University. He was a close friend and associate of Helen Schucman and William Thetford, the two people whose joining together was the immediate stimulus for the scribing of A Course in Miracles. Kenneth has been involved with A Course in Miracles since 1973, writing, teaching, and integrating its principles with his practice of psychotherapy. He is on the Executive Board of the Foundation for Inner Peace, publishers of A Course in Miracles.*

In 1983, with his wife Gloria, he began the Foundation for A Course in Miracles, and in 1984 this evolved into a Teaching and Healing Center in Crompond, New York, which was quickly outgrown. In 1988 they opened the Academy and Retreat Center in upstate New York. In 1995 they began the Institute for Teaching Inner Peace through A Course in Miracles, an educational corporation chartered by the New York State Board of Regents. In 2001 the Foundation moved to Temecula, California. The Foundation publishes a quarterly newsletter, "The Lighthouse," which is available free of charge. The following is Kenneth and Gloria's vision of the Foundation.

In our early years of studying *A Course in Miracles,* as well as teaching and applying its principles in our respective professions of psychotherapy, and teaching and school administration, it seemed evident that this was not the simplest of thought systems to understand. This was so not only in the intellectual grasp of its teachings, but perhaps more importantly in the application of these teachings to our personal lives. Thus, it appeared to us from the beginning that the Course lent itself to teaching, parallel to the ongoing teachings of the Holy Spirit in the daily opportunities within our relationships, which are discussed in the early pages of the manual for teachers.

One day several years ago while Helen Schucman and I (Kenneth) were discussing these ideas, she shared a vision that she had had of a teaching center as a white temple with a gold cross atop it. Although it was clear that this image was symbolic, we understood it to be representative of what the teaching center was to be: a place where the person of Jesus and his message in *A Course in Miracles* would be manifest. We have sometimes seen an image of a lighthouse shining its light into the sea, calling to it those passers-by who sought it. For us, this light is the Course's teaching of forgiveness, which we would hope to share with those who are drawn to the Foundation's form of teaching and its vision of *A Course in Miracles*.

This vision entails the belief that Jesus gave the Course at this particular time in this particular form for several reasons. These include:

1) the necessity of healing the mind of its belief that attack is salvation; this is accomplished through forgiveness, the undoing of our belief in the reality of separation and guilt.

2) emphasizing the importance of Jesus and/or the Holy Spirit as our loving and gentle Teacher, and developing a personal relationship with this Teacher.

3) correcting the errors of Christianity, particularly where it has emphasized suffering, sacrifice, separation, and sacrament as being inherent in God's plan for salvation.

Our thinking has always been inspired by Plato (and his mentor Socrates), both the man and his teachings. Plato's Academy was a place where serious and thoughtful people came to study his philosophy in an atmosphere conducive to their learning, and then returned to their professions to implement what they were taught by the great philosopher. Thus, by integrating abstract philosophical ideals with experience, Plato's school seemed to be the perfect model for the teaching center that we directed for so many years.

We therefore see the Foundation's principal purpose as being to help students of *A Course in Miracles* deepen their understanding of its thought system, conceptually and experientially, so that they may be more effective instruments of Jesus' teaching in their own lives. Since teaching forgiveness without experiencing it is empty, one of the Foundation's specific goals is to help facilitate the process whereby people may be better able to know that their own sins are forgiven and that they are truly loved by God. Thus is the Holy Spirit able to extend His Love through them to others.

Foundation for A COURSE IN MIRACLES®
Temecula, California

Please see our Web site, www.facim.org, for a complete listing of publications and available translations. You may also write, or call our office for information:

Foundation for A Course in Miracles®
41397 Buecking Drive
Temecula, CA 92590
(951) 296-6261 • fax (951) 296-5455